STRAIGHT FROM THE HEART

WHAT KEEPS WEC GOING AND GROWING?

STRAIGHT FROM THE HEART

A symposium by various
WEC contributors

compiled

by

Evan Davies and Stewart Dinnen

Acknowledgements

This book is a joint effort. Many people have worked to bring it to fulfilment. There is a small army of writers who have shared their experience and wisdom. Stewart Dinnen worked hard with me to shape it while Daphne Spraggett used her considerable skills to refine it. Wellspring Media (WEC UK), Christian Focus Publications and several friends have given time and effort to see it into production. The WEC International Publications Committee gave encouragement over several years.

Thank you each one.

Evan Davies

Published by WEC Publications, Bulstrode, Gerrards Cross, Bucks, SL9 8SZ, England

First Edition 2004

ISBN 0 900828 85 4

Cover by June Marshall

Design and layout by Bernard White, Dartford, Kent

Contents

Each chapter is followed by a living example of the Core Value explained.

Foreword

WEC started with a man, and the man became a mission. It would be so easy for the mission to become just a movement, and the movement a monument – finally, perhaps, to be only a memory!

So what is needed to keep a mission going, growing, and advancing? We believe it is loyalty to basic biblical principles, plus a readiness to be responsive and adaptable to changing conditions and needs, or, as one field leader has put it, 'solid at the core, fluid at the edges'.

If there is to be dynamic development, new strategies must meet areas of need. Old formulas certainly cannot be jettisoned but change allows new values to be articulated and adopted. The real challenge is in holding these core principles together.

WEC started as a mission in 1913. Its founder, C.T. Studd, was an enthusiast for God who laid down single-eyed principles for the organisation. He called them 'The Five Smooth Stones' (after David's ammunition in his fight against Goliath). They were:

1. Absolute faith in the deity of each person in the Trinity.
2. Absolute belief in the full inspiration of the Old and New Testament scriptures.
3. Vow to know and to preach none other save Jesus Christ and Him crucified.
4. Obedience to Christ's command to love all who love the Lord Jesus sincerely, without partiality, and to love all people.
5. Absolute faith in the will, power and providence of God to meet our every need in His service.

It had a rocky ride in those early days and it took a split in 1931 for the young mission to be convinced that fellowship had to be a foundation principle as well.

For the mission to be effective, spiritual power was needed in the lives of its members. Norman Grubb was used by God to show that a grasp of union with Christ in His death, burial and resurrection provided the key to both godly living and effective service.

So as the mission grew, four principles came to dominate its life: **FAITH** in God to supply all needs, **HOLINESS** as a practical outworking of a relationship with God, **SACRIFICE** as the inevitable cost involved in reaching the unevangelised and **FELLOWSHIP** which is the under-pinning of mutual care and concern that holds us together.

As the years have gone on, leaders have changed, the numbers of workers, fields and sending bases have multiplied, and other useful principles have emerged and been adopted.

This book is about the things that are the heartbeat of WEC International today. It isn't that we've arrived – there's still a long way to go – but we want to share with you some things that we have learnt and are still learning.

Thank you to all who have contributed and helped in this compilation, especially my good friend and mentor Stewart Dinnen, who went to his reward before the book was published. He was a good man, full of faith and the Holy Spirit. We miss him.

For the sake of a lost world and the growing church,

Evan Davies
International Director
WEC International 2004

Introduction
The Start and the Heart

WEC Motto:

If Jesus Christ be God and died for me, then no sacrifice can be too great for me to make for Him!

Words of a fanatic? Or a pious sentiment without practical application? No!

A young man asked C.T. Studd, 'Is it a fact that at fifty-two you mean to leave your country, your home, your wife and your children?' 'What?' he responded, 'Have you been talking of the sacrifice of the Lord Jesus Christ tonight? If Jesus Christ be God and died for me then no sacrifice can be too great for me to make for Him!' This response epitomised his commitment over the remaining eighteen years of his life and became the motto of the fledgling mission. The ringing words catch the imagination, say what the heart is thinking and seek to express an inner conviction and throbbing desire to serve such a Master.

This motto has been the inspiration behind the testimonies, sometimes wonderful yet often terrible, exciting yet sometimes tragic, of several thousands of missionaries who have served the King of Kings in the ranks of WEC.

CT (as Studd was affectionately known) was in Liverpool in 1908 when he saw an advertisement for a meeting: *Cannibals want missionaries!* Amused, he had entered the building and been challenged to his depths by the great explorer, Karl Kumm. According to Kumm, explorers, big-game hunters, traders and scientists had all crossed the 'black' continent, yet there was no Christian there telling them of Jesus. The shame sank into CT's soul and he responded.

Broken in health, penniless and with no supporting mission, he stepped out in faith, staking his all on God's promises. He wrote at that time: 'My soul is on fire to do the work of Christ. I seem to hear Jesus saying, "Go over and possess the good land of the world. Every place your foot shall tread upon (thank God I have large ones!) to you have I given it."' He had a burning, consuming desire to live for Christ and the world.

He wrote to his dear wife, 'I think, and think, and think, all upon the same line – a new crusade. Things simply surge through my mind and head, and God speaks to me every time I lie down, and assures me that He is going to do a wonderful work.'

From that small beginning – CT, the pioneer, going out to Central Africa while his wife stayed at home caring for the infant mission and calling others to join its ranks – has blossomed the WEC of today. Now about 2,000 strong and working in more than seventy countries around the world, it still has the same fervour, the same objective of bringing lost souls to Christ, then establishing them in Him and in His Word, till they too are willing to give their all in serving Him, 'Whom to serve is perfect freedom.'

The ringing words of that motto have spurred many of us, not only to join the team but also to keep going when the way seemed impossible, or lonely, or frustrating, or dangerous, or even pointless. Dear Jessie Scholes, who had worked alongside CT in the 1920s, was still trekking the forest paths of Congo when over eighty years of age. Despite being widowed and having undergone surgery for cancer of the gall-bladder, she continued to preach the gospel in scattered villages until the Lord called her home; Bill McChesney, still in his twenties, with a boyish grin and an irrepressible love for children, was gunned down by savage guerrilla soldiers in Congo. And many, many others have been spurred on by the same challenge that 'If Jesus Christ be God and died for me, then no sacrifice can be too great for me to make for Him!'

After founding the new mission in 1913, CT wrote a series of booklets blazing with Christ's passion for the lost. They were a call to arms to countless men and women. '*We should* go crusading for Christ,' he wrote. 'We have the men, the means and the ways – steam and electricity and iron have levelled the lands and bridged the seas. The doors of the world have been opened wide for us by our God. We pray and preach; we bow the knee; we are optimists everyone; we shout "Onward, Christian soldiers, marching as to war" … and then? … and then? … we whisper, "I pray You have me excused!" What glorious humbugs we are!'

And today, we live in an age of telecommunications unknown in any previous era; we can send messages to one another as fast as blinking an eye; we can cross the oceans between breakfast and lunch; we have everything that we could possibly need to do the task. We have fantastic tools for helping us in learning languages and in translating the scriptures. Missionary training colleges abound on every continent to prepare us for the task of living cross-culturally. Yet …?

CT spoke of 500 millions yet to be evangelised – today that number is nearer three billion. If the task was urgent eighty years ago, it is far more urgent today! CT wrote: 'Believing that further delay would be sinful, some of God's insignificants and nobodies in particular, are trusting in an omnipotent God and have decided on certain simple lines, according to the Book of God, to make a definite attempt to make the evangelisation of the world an accomplished fact. For this purpose we have banded ourselves under the name of "Christ's etceteras" – we are merely nobodies ….' It was to them he gave the mission motto:

If Jesus Christ be God and died for me, then no sacrifice can be too great for me to make for Him!

This motto has scorched many hearts and minds from that time to this. It gives us the **Why?** of WEC as to our purpose, our commission, our stated aims in our *Principles and Practice* – our need to obey God's clear command to go and tell all ethnic groups the Good News, to share His loving compassion with the needy peoples of the world, and to draw them together to establish fellowships in which they will live and witness for Him in their own communities.

It gives us the **What?** of WEC, as to our presentation of the message of redeeming love through our daily life-style – by a willingness to live sacrificially, in total dependence on God for all our needs, seeking the Holy Spirit's enabling to be holy, and to work in harmony one with another, 'each esteeming others better than themselves'.

They give us the **How?** of WEC, as to how we seek to put into practice our convictions – preaching the gospel of our Lord Jesus Christ true to His written Word; praying in faith, believing for the salvation of all peoples; working in unity with all others who hold the same high view of scripture.

The heart of the motto can best be captured by one more quotation from CT at the time of the birth of WEC. This will answer the question **Who?**

The Christian Evangelist must be a man of God and a child of man. He is not the salaried servant of the Mission Committee. He is a servant of Jesus Christ with Whom he has settled terms of agreement already. He knows no other Master … If death overtakes him on the battlefield, he knows such to be a special mark of Christ's favour, Who has thus honoured and promoted him sooner than he had any right to expect. As he looks to God to supply his needs, so also shall he look to God for his guidance and shall obey Him.

Too long have we been waiting for one another to begin! The time for waiting is past! The hour of God has struck! War is declared! In God's holy Name, let us arise and build! We will dare to trust our God, we will venture our all for Him, we will live and we will die for Him, and we will do it with His joy unspeakable singing aloud in our hearts. We will a thousand times rather die trusting only in our God than live trusting in man. And when we come to this position the battle is already won, and the end of the glorious campaign is in sight.

Oh, that this motto may ring again, loud and clear, as a clarion call to many more to join the ranks of WEC International, to serve such a wonderful and worthy Master wherever and whenever He chooses to send them, to do whatever He asks of them, not counting the cost but rejoicing in the privilege!

Helen Roseveare

Do it Now!

Evan Davies with John Bardsley

Core Value: *To bring the gospel of our Lord Jesus Christ to the remaining unevangelised peoples with the utmost urgency*

It is no mistake that we are called Worldwide Evangelization for Christ (WEC). Our over-riding purpose and passion is to see Jesus known everywhere where He is not yet known.

When C.T. Studd set up camp at Niangara and then at Nala and Ibambi in the Congo, he had one aim and that was to share the liberating gospel of Jesus with people who needed to be set free. He said 'Some want to live within the sound of church and chapel bell, I want to run a rescue shop within a yard of hell.' He spent the rest of his life with this burning passion. Some have said he gambled and lost, but one year after his death 7,000 Christians came together for a Christian conference. His vision spurred thousands to commit themselves to Christ's service. The new mission spread to Latin America, the Middle East, Asia and West Africa. From there it has gone to Southern Europe, South, East and Central Asia.

The aim wasn't to go to the most responsive peoples but to the least evangelised – to give them the opportunity to hear why Jesus came and why He had to die. So at strategic times in WEC history, a fresh survey has been made of the places which have been least evangelised and a commitment made to believe for recruits and the means of entry.

Over the years we have become involved in medical, agricultural and literacy work, as well as other humanitarian aid ministries. But, as one of our colleagues has said, 'Going to bed hungry is not the worst! Waking up in hell is.' The spiritual battle is the core battle. Jesus came not for good people but for sinners, for the ones who are perishing (John 3:16) so that they might hear, repent and believe. Of course we have to respect people of other faiths, but we have to recognise that there is only one Name given to men through whom we must be saved (Acts 4:12) and so, in humility and boldness, we have an obligation to share the Good News of Jesus. He was concerned for the 'sheep who are not in this sheepfold' (John 10:16 GNB) that they might have overflowing life (John 10:10).

His instructions are that we must witness, make disciples and preach the gospel in all the world.

WEC workers have been responding to Christ's call for about ninety years. The stories of responses are thrilling; hundreds of thousands have turned to Christ and become a part of His church.

As a boy in the 1950s, Evan remembers praying every Friday night for the people of Burkina Faso and for Jack Robertson who was working among the Lobi tribe where the power of the fetish held thousands in cruel slavery. At that time the church was so small the believers could be counted on one hand. Today the church there is about 10,000 strong. Elaine Crane and Beth Allinger spent many years reaching out to Nepalese young people in Assam and discipling them. Today there are about 500,000 Nepalese believers. Even though the work in Japan has been hard and unresponsive, about twenty WEC-related churches testify to the power of the Spirit to bring freedom and new life. In a restricted access nation cell churches have mushroomed as young people have found Jesus to be the answer to their spiritual needs. And we could go on ...

It's not fair!

John Bardsley, International Director for Prayer, tells how he heard about the need and why he believes the task is achievable:

I was nineteen, a student teacher, when I told God 'My life is no good to me the way it is. If you can do anything with it, you can have it.' I knew I was not my own any more! Immediately He showed me that ten per cent of Christian workers are reaching out to ninety per cent of the world's population, and said, 'Go help carry the heavy end.' Imagine a refugee camp where the first three rows are fed three times a day, the next four rows once a week, and the last three rows not at all! That's how we have obeyed the command to make the gospel available to every person (Mark 16:15). Thirty per cent have the gospel every Sunday if they wish. Forty per cent have some access to it, though with difficulty. And thirty per cent have no access whatever! It's not fair! RUN! Reach the Unevangelised Now!

It's all promised!

It's going to happen! Revelation 5:9 and 7:9 both record John's prophecy that it will happen. He said, 'I saw people from every tribe, language, ethnic group and nation in heaven, clothed in the glistening purity of Jesus, exulting in worship around the throne.' Countless millions of us! If it's going to happen anyway, and we are the agents to make it happen, why can't it happen sooner rather than later? Don't you want Jesus to return in your lifetime? I do. I don't want to die, I want to fly!

We have the technology

Winston Churchill, Prime Minister of UK in the second World War, said, 'Give us the tools and we will finish the job.' God has given us the tools today to evangelise the world. Air travel shrank the globe ages ago. Computers make translation so much faster. E-mail keeps isolated missionaries in touch. Hand-wound and solar-powered cassette players and radio receivers take the message where batteries are too expensive. Christian radio blankets the globe. The *Jesus* film is the most-watched, most-translated movie on earth. Satellite TV beams the Good News, unjammable, right into Middle Eastern homes. Smart cards repeat scripture recordings. Teleconferencing facilities mean an evangelist like Billy Graham can preach in 3,000 cities simultaneously.

We have the spiritual authority

Spiritually there are all the resources necessary to build the kingdom. Jesus said, 'If you love me, obey what I command.' But with that command He also promised, 'Ask anything in my name and I will do it' (John 14:14-15). Before He sent His disciples out to preach, He gave them authority over all the power of the enemy (Luke 9:1 and 10:19). He has given us the authority with the command: 'All authority in heaven and earth has been given to me, so go make disciples in every ethnic group on earth' (Matthew 28:19, free translation). What's stopping us?

We can see the finishing line!

Two thousand million people make up the 2,915 ethnic groups that still have no viable church of their own (i.e. with less than two per cent of the population evangelical). The Joshua Project lists 1,522 of these with over 10,000 in population. One example of these is the Hindu-speaking peoples of North India. There are over 200 million of them in 6,400 castes. Only 100 castes have any Christians at all. By 1998 all but 200 of these ethnic groups listed by the Joshua Project had been 'claimed' – they are in the loving plans of some church or mission somewhere.

After that there is one more list, of all the tiny people groups. There may be up to 2,397 of them. Many of them are formed when fragments of larger peoples are cut off through migration or by fleeing as refugees. Others are secluded in some remote area, still waiting. For example, in the south-west of Burkina Faso there are 8,000 Kaan, 5,500 Black Dogosé, 3,500 Khisa, 1,500 Tenbo, and 600 Gbadogo. Among the Kaan there are 120 believers, among the Black Dogosé only six, the Khisa fifteen, the Tenbo none at all, and the Gbadogo fifteen. The Lord God loves them all, and has committed to WEC the task of establishing His church among them. These 2,397 peoples are the last unreached peoples on earth! When we've reached these, we've reached the last of the unreached people groups!

The financial and personnel resources do exist

All we need are the people to send, the money to keep them there, and the prayer to break down the barriers! Does that sound familiar? The good news is that there are 600 evangelical churches for every ethnic group without a church.

So – what are we waiting for?

It's worth it!

Dave Macmillan

Fifteen hundred lovers of Jesus. That is reason to celebrate! And that's what we did on 2 May 1998.

The event was WEC's fiftieth anniversary in the North Thailand provinces of Tak, Kamphaengphet, and Sukhothai. When Wilf Overgaard and his tiny pioneer team broke into this area in 1948, there was not one known Christian. When he returned to the place of beginnings at the celebration of thanksgiving, he was greeted by a crowd representing seventy Thai and Karen churches. Past and present walked together down memory lane. Old and new believers met, city and rural churches bonded, and a dozen missionary 'oldies' came back for the big day.

It was more than a celebration of the past; it was a springboard for the future. It was a call for a new generation of pioneers. One hundred and fifty missionaries, past and present, together with local believers have paid the sower's price to prepare the field for a greater harvest. The celebration day climaxed with many of the Thai, Thai-Chinese and Karen Christians standing together with missionaries from twelve nations and asking God to use them as harvesters in this ripe field. 'Harvest Joy' was the theme of the day.

The scene changes to the General Conference of the Evangelical Fellowship of Thailand attended by 300 leaders representing churches countrywide. At the coffee break, a middle-aged pastor from a small town in Thailand's northern-most province came up to me. I had never seen him before. He lifted his hands and gave me a Thai greeting. His eyes locked on to mine as he spoke: 'I just wanted to say thank you. Thank you for leaving your nation to come and bless mine.' I wanted to embrace him, to tell him I have received more than I have given up, to tell him how much I love his nation, to tell him how I long to be a bigger blessing.

2

Heart and Hands

Phyllis Kilbourn

Core Value: *To demonstrate the compassion of Christ to a needy world.*

Hearts were deeply moved as Phyllis Kilbourn told the delegates at WEC's international leaders' conference in 1996 of the plight of millions of children and young people around the world, unevangelised, abused, neglected and abandoned by society in general and, in large measure, by the church. There was an immediate decision to set up a new ministry within WEC called Rainbows of Hope to reach children with the love of Jesus.

'Clothe yourselves with compassion.' What does this mean? It's broader than a specific function like evangelism or social action, and it goes much deeper than an emotion or feeling. When Christ ministered, He met the needs of hurting people – not simply by social action (as in feeding the 5,000) or proclaiming the Good News, but through a synthesis of both. These functions were inter-dependent and could not be separated without diluting the effectiveness of His ministry. Through compassionate caring, He prepared hearts to respond to His message.

Compassion must first be transferred to us from the One who is described as 'full of compassion' (James 5:11). Only when we feel Christ's pain for a broken and fallen world are we ready to fulfil His mandate to transfer His compassion in redemptive ways to the lost. A holistic ministry that demonstrates Christ's love in practical ways will prepare hearts to receive the gospel.

Different viewpoints inspire different approaches. There are those who are fervently committed to the task of world evangelisation and church-planting goals. There are those whose hearts break for hurting humanity where deep emotional wounding, poverty and exploitation reveal mankind's wretchedness.

Although WEC has traditionally been a church-planting mission, the heart of WEC's core value of compassion can be likened to an old song which proclaims, 'Love and marriage go together like a horse and carriage.' Today, more than ever, compassionate ministry and worldwide evangelisation must go together.

Care of the needy

Jesus cared for children. He had compassion on the woman of Nain who had lost her only son (Luke 7:11-17). Verse 13 says that 'When the Lord saw her, his heart went out to her and he said, "Don't cry."' Knowing the value of children in the home and the mother-love bond, Jesus could identify with the mother's pain. He responded to her pain with a life-giving touch that restored the son to his mother. He tenderly referred to Jairus's daughter, who also needed a life-giving touch, as 'my child' (Luke 9:54).

Compassion replaces cruelty

In WEC's earliest days in the Congo, team members, appalled by the cruelty to children who became child-brides, opened the mission station as a house of refuge for them. Fulani was one of them. Twice she ran away to escape her old, ill-kempt, cruel husband but was recaptured, brutally beaten and maimed. Edith Moules records the story:

> First he tied her wrists together very tightly with strong native rope, and then he suspended the shrieking child by the ends of that rope to the rafters of the roof of an old hut. But this was not all. He beat the little wriggling form with a whip, and left her hanging there for two whole nights. She was taken down at last and the burst, bleeding and suppurating arms were bound up native fashion, but later one hand sloughed right off at the wrist and the other was shrunken and twisted out of shape permanently through the pressure on the nerves.

Another expression of compassion was to those who had contracted leprosy. They, like AIDS/HIV victims today, were the outcasts of society. Their dwellings were considered off-limits and their children were refused acceptance in local schools and communities. Edith Moules recalls her struggles in initiating a ministry to them:

> It was night-time. The shutters were open, letting in the moonlight and the many forest sounds; yet it was quiet, or as quiet as an African night can be. But it was not quiet in my own heart, for these words were speaking loudly, 'Who is my neighbour?' And the only picture I could conjure up was of a black man, not young, covered in sores, having lost most of his toes, his face puffed and bloated with disease, who had arrived at my house a few days previously with a tiny bundle of belongings wrapped up in a banana leaf and slung on a stick over his shoulder, solemnly announcing that he had come. He had come, walking on those poor feet about 130 kilometres, because he had heard that someone was there giving medicine to sick people. He was a leper.

As Edith resisted paying the price of compassion for these people, the words, 'Who is my neighbour?' continued to clamour for an answer. She finally understood the call of God. She stated, 'It was not until I realised that the leper was my neighbour that I could get peace.' The matter settled, Edith began to take action and soon the Mabese Centre became a place of healing and hope for hundreds of Congo's outcasts.

No wonder a healthy church developed in these areas! Christ's love demonstrated through care for their desperate physical needs opened hearts to His redemptive love.

Compassion for children

WEC workers, Andy and Sylvia Lawrance, opened their hearts to the street children in Brazil. They started a home where children such as Jorge could be helped. After Jorge had received large doses of loving care, Andy could report:

> He is the most changed boy around. A street kid, accustomed to lying with a straight face, stealing while he's talking to you, being a perfect gentleman when it's to his advantage, and being put on probation for threatening to kill a school teacher, we are seeing changes in his life! All of a sudden he decided to study seriously. He was even made class representative. His marks are improving. He is now working on the smaller press in our printshop.

In country after country millions of children are suffering from a multitude of exploitative and abusive situations: living on danger-filled city streets, participating in the horrors of warfare, existing in extreme poverty, forced into the slavery of child labour, humiliated by degrading sexual exploitation, ravaged by AIDS/HIV, mutilated or disabled through natural disasters. Many children come from fractured, abusive or dysfunctional families who are also in critical need of compassionate ministry.

When the disciples tried to prevent children from coming to Him, Jesus rebuked them. His invitation revealed the importance of children in Christ's kingdom and gave a beautiful dignity to childhood. The message was clear: children are precious, worthy of blessing, ministry, and respect. Rainbows of Hope, a ministry to children in crisis, is committed to demonstrate this.

Compassion through medicine and rehabilitation

David Barron and his wife, Margaret, were WEC's first missionaries in The Gambia, West Africa. When David died, it seemed that the door into that country had closed. But God sent a small team of German nurses to initiate what has become a network of clinics and service ministries throughout the country. Each year tens of thousands of patients are treated, literacy classes are held, a study centre is used by hundreds of children, and skill centres, where women are taught typing and sewing, are in operation. Churches have come into being through practical care and compassion.

Medical ministries are proving their worth in Africa, Asia and the Middle East. In environments which are often inhospitable, team members are demonstrating the love of God in ways that people can see – babies delivered, eyes treated, wounds attended and the sick served in Christ's name.

In many countries teams of workers are involved in extending a hand to those who have been trapped through drugs. Significant love has impacted many lives and today hundreds have found freedom in Christ and have been linked to new churches which are the outcome of this ministry.

Whether it is in running day schools, improving gardens, developing literacy programmes, providing relief and development or cattle for those who have lost all they had, WEC teams are sharing Christ's love around the world. It is tough, often thankless, but so relevant and necessary. Some of the workers involved are highly trained professionals, others with hearts filled with love do what they can – just like Mary did for Jesus (Mark 14:6-8).

The challenge

Are the suffering, exploited and poverty-stricken to be left in their brokenness and despair? Those like fourteen-year-old Juliet, trying to rear three younger siblings in the worst slum in Manila where prostitution is the only way to earn money for food and medicine? Or like Junior, conscripted into the Liberian army as a child soldier at eight years of age who, after three years of indiscriminate killings, states he has nothing more to live for? Or like Sergei, who has only a sewer pipe to call home and must sniff glue to keep away the pangs of hunger?

'Is there no balm in Gilead? Is there no physician there?' cried Jeremiah. He knew that healing for broken people was possible. He knew God's name is Jehovah Rapha – the God who heals. He knew that there was no wound or hurt so great, so horrible, so devastating or destructive that our sovereign God could not heal, but He uses human instruments in the process.

Our hearts are challenged and stirred. It is through Christ's compassion for a needy world that WEC is committed to ministries that lead people to Jesus through passionate care and godly living.

AIDS: it affects us all

Dr Gisela Schneider

She was only nine years old when I first met her. Fatou* was a shy little girl. Nobody sent her to school. Fees were a problem, and her mother was very ill. Fatou never knew who her father was. She received very little love and care.

One day as we sat in the little mud house belonging to Fatou's grandfather, he told us that we could have his sick daughter, and her three children ages six, eight and ten. Perplexed and overwhelmed, I knew I could not take on such a responsibility myself. I called our church leaders who felt strongly that we should take up the challenge to care for both the mother and the children. Fatou's mother had made a commitment to Christ, and the church was her family now.

The first problem was schooling for the children, but where and how? We found a local school for the boy and were able to enrol the girls in a Christian boarding school. What a privilege! The mother made a remarkable recovery in spite of her HIV status. Health-wise and faith-wise she stood her ground. She was going to be a Christian, and nothing would divert her. One day, Fatou returned from boarding school telling us that she had given her life to Christ. This was a bold step in a Muslim area. Later her mother wanted the girls back home with her. We were sad to see them leave boarding school, but they had at least learned some educational basics to continue in the public educational system.

For over four years we have cared for this family so infected and affected by HIV/AIDS. We have had our ups and down, but overall we have seen what a difference care and support can make, not only to the patient, but also to the children who are equally affected by the situation. The question remains, 'What will happen when mom is gone?'

However, for Fatou it means that right now most of the household chores rest on her young fourteen-year-old shoulders – not a rare situation in sub-Saharan Africa where more than twelve million children are orphaned by HIV/AIDS.

There are no easy answers to the HIV dilemma, but Immanuel means 'GOD with us' – even in the midst of a pandemic of unprecedented proportions. By HIS grace we can make a difference in the lives of people, communities and a suffering world.

*Not her real name

Babe, I love drugs more than I love you

Angelo Gargiulo is thirty-seven years old and lives in one of the towns at the foot of the famous Mount Vesuvius in Italy. His parents were ordinary working class folk who prided themselves in being law-abiding citizens. However, times were hard and his parents struggled to care for their eight children so they gave Angelo, the youngest of the family, to an aunt and uncle.

Angelo's story is translated by Lindsay McKenzie.

My adoptive parents were the exact opposite of my natural parents. My uncle practised black magic and had lots of money. Fascinated by his affluence and his occult powers, I left school at fifteen years of age and learnt business techniques and how to practise black magic from him. Soon I became wealthy in my own right and thought I'd reached Utopia. I did everything I could to throw off the memories of my younger years as the son of working class parents. Far from being a well-behaved and meek guy, my new lifestyle made me proud, arrogant and sophisticated.

My uncle had close relatives who were known and feared *mafiosi* in my hometown. They also trafficked in illegal drugs. If I had been impressed by my uncle's well-to-do lifestyle, I was even more impressed with how these cousins-by-marriage lived and operated. I decided that their way of living was what I wanted too.

My first experience with narcotics was an all-night affair with women and cocaine. After a few months of regular cocaine use, I began to sniff heroin. I kept up this cycle of drugs, women and vice for a number of years without too many negative effects.

However, once I'd entered into the heroin phase, relationships with my closest friends gradually began to grow cold. They disappeared completely when I became a chronic user, hooked on heroin. Even my relationship with my fiancée was in deep crisis. Finally I broke it off with her, casually announcing to her one day that I loved heroin more than I loved her. I'd even lost the ability to smile.

I searched for other alternatives to heroin, and began to inject psychiatric drugs, methadone or, when none of these were available, hard liquor. I drank gin from morning to night. I was useless for any type of work. I just existed.

Thanks to the insistence of my brother, I returned with him to the Betel centre. I had been there before for an interview; this time I stayed. I felt that my life was constantly surrounded by deep darkness that blinded me from seeing reality. I

Continued

arrived at the men's residence one evening and while I waited for them to check through all my personal effects (for drugs or forbidden objects) I suddenly felt an uncanny peace within me and saw a bright light all around me.

Soon I realised that although the other guys were just like me, they practised a totally different set of values. They said that they had learnt them from reading the Bible. 'Drug users reading the Bible?' I mused. Eventually I began to understand why they lived and talked as they did.

I began to take notice of what God's voice was saying to me. It was not a literal, audible voice, but rather a voice deep inside me which spoke to my innermost being. As I listened to that voice I began to realise that only Jesus could fill the great void that this world and its particular values had created in me over the years – a void which I had tried desperately to fill with drugs, women, money and the like.

I have decided to follow Jesus with all my heart and I consider myself to be blessed in every sense of the word. Not only have I stopped taking drugs but I am aware that God has transformed me. Even though I am the same Angelo Gargiulo, I know I am a new person!

3

Sow the Seed; Nurture the Plants

Brian Woodford

Core Value: *To plant churches and lead them to spiritual maturity*

In the years since 1913 WEC workers have been used by God to start many churches. In the Congo there are hundreds, in Asia small cell groups and churches, and in countries like Uruguay and Venezuela the mission team has withdrawn because its work was done. In many places churches have been set up and authority transferred into local hands.

The groups planted by an interdenominational organisation have an incredible opportunity to get down to basics. What is the real church? How does it run? What organisational pattern should it follow?

As a pioneer church planter in Burkina Faso, I wrestled with these issues. There are crucial principles in the job of making disciples and birthing the church. Taking the gospel to the remaining unreached peoples of the world is only the beginning. Our real aim is to plant churches because that is where disciples grow to maturity. 'Make disciples of all nations, baptising them … teaching them to obey everything I have commanded you' (Matthew 28:19-20). We are immediately struck by the simplicity of the words in contrast to the complexity of carrying them out!

Preparation and privilege

There is, broadly speaking, a need for two types of training, one theological and the other anthropological. The first need of a church planter is to have a deep understanding of the message he wishes to bring and to see it demonstrated in the way he or she lives. The second need is an ability to communicate this message in a form that will be understood by his hearers. Neither objective is likely to be achieved in a weekend of training!

What a privilege it is to spread the incredibly Good News of Jesus among people who are hearing it for the first time! The only greater joy is to witness the first believers turning to the Lord. And then they discover that you are a brother, or a sister, and that there is a whole new family into which they have been born. That makes it all worthwhile.

The wise church planter always remembers that the Holy Spirit lives within the newest believer just as much as He lives in the missionary. This means that the foreigner doesn't have to have all the answers. God hears the praises of spiritual babies, and He answers their prayers too. He also gives them gifts of His grace so that they can begin to function together as His temple, each having something special to contribute.

The purposes of the church

God has called the church into being
- to worship the King,
- to proclaim the Kingdom,
- to demonstrate that Kingdom.

To put this another way, we can say that the church is created to be a temple of the Holy Spirit, a herald of the Word of God, and a servant of Christ in the world.

Worship

The biblical picture is far more than singing our praises on a Sunday morning, although it includes that. Worship, in a biblical sense, touches every area of our lives. Wherever you find a people totally sold out to the purposes of God for their lives, there you find enjoyable worship. Wherever there is shallowness in commitment, Sunday worship invariably falls flat. True worship is the overflow of a life given over to God.

I shall never forget the depth of genuine praise that I found in Spain one Sunday morning as a group of converted drug addicts sang their hearts out to the Lord. He had done something for them. Their lives had been turned around. The worship came from the heart. Today this church is the largest evangelical fellowship in Madrid. How did it all begin?

New missionaries Elliott Tepper (from USA) and Lindsay McKenzie (from Australia) thought they could reach the university students of Madrid, but they found them unresponsive.

They resorted to street meetings in the lower class suburb of San Blas, but only drug addicts stood around. They prayed, 'Lord, send us some normal people!' But none came. Then they realised, during protracted times of prayer, that God was commissioning them to start a drug rehabilitation programme as a key to church planting.

Lindsay took pity on one hopeless character and gave him a bed in his own apartment. Within a week he was soundly converted. Soon Lindsay had eight fellows with him – and that was too much for the neighbours in the block!

God provided a run-down property near Barachas airport – and that was the start of the Betel church.

Proclamation

What does it mean to proclaim the kingdom? It means finding ways to bring the gospel to the lost. But it also means that believers will be taught the Scriptures from cover to cover. There are not two messages, one for the unconverted and another for the Christian. There is really only one message, and that is Christ.

In order to communicate this message to an unreached people group there is often the initial challenge of making the Scriptures available in a language that can be understood. That is what church planting meant for me. How long did it take? About ten years to learn the language and many more to translate the New Testament. In some places the Scriptures are already available, but most times the church planter still has to learn the language. That is why we want those who will come for the long term.

But something more is needed before the church can be said to be established. 'Reliable men' must be trained so that they in turn can teach others (2 Tim. 2:2). The newly emerging church must be challenged to take the Word of God to others who have not heard. In Ghana this became a joint project, as teams of both expatriate and Ghanaian missionaries were formed to plant churches among language groups that had not yet been reached. In Congo, Bantu pastors and evangelists have committed themselves full-time to church planting among the many scattered pygmy groups. In Thailand one team member produced a multi-volume comprehensive Bible teaching course designed specifically with the Thai culture in mind.

Service

The third function of the church is service. The church is called to *demonstrate* the kingdom. Unless our message becomes visible it lacks credibility. Churches that live out their message really make an impact. I think of churches in the deprived areas of Bogotá, Colombia, that are open day after day to provide a hot meal for kids who would otherwise be roaming the streets. Across the globe there are English language classes, computer courses, orphanages, drug rehabilitation programmes, medical clinics – all providing tangible evidence of the love of God in Christ to those who wouldn't think of coming to a church meeting.

Strike the right strategy

Think of the church as having five rooms. There is the Family Room which emphasises the spiritual nature of the church as the people of God, the body of Christ. The Administration Room which reminds us that the church needs structure and leadership. The third room we might call the Worship Room, reminding us of the church as the temple of the Holy Spirit. The Message Room represents the church as a herald, commissioned to take the Word of God to those outside the church and to teach it to those within. Lastly there is the Service Room making the Good News visible to the world.

Any of the five rooms may become the point of attraction. Often in a Muslim context it is the Service Room that provides the focal point for contact. Where public evangelism is possible, it is often the Herald Room that brings people in.

The Cell Church approach, which is now being adopted in a variety of formats by churches all over the world, makes excellent use of the Family Room. Similarly, in Alpha groups non-Christians are welcomed into a small group of like-minded people and are able to explore the basics of the gospel in a non-threatening environment. In many Latin American countries the Worship Room provides the shop window as people are drawn into the dynamic (and noisy!) celebration-type services that reflect a radical devotion to Christ. On the other hand, for those brought up in Christian families it is often the very organisation of the church – the Administration Room – that provides their first experience of church life.

There are many ways into the church! Any one of these five rooms can lead to a living encounter with the Lord Jesus. And having entered by one door, the seeker needs to be introduced, step by step, into the other rooms. They are all a part of the biblical church. And the church planter will want to lay a foundation for them all.

WEC has a specific goal to see churches come into being as a result of all that we do. It's the church of the living God that will stand against the gates of hell and that will continue to spread the Good News long after a cross-cultural worker has gone. Even though the task is a greatly challenging one and full of difficulties, it is the greatest legacy we can leave to the people we are privileged to serve.

By all means

Patrick McElligott with Stewart Dinnen

Experienced missionaries, Patrick and Sarah McElligott, were thoroughly discouraged. They had been in Ishiyama (central Japan) for a year, yet no one had been converted. Then disaster struck.

Patrick takes up the story.

About 11pm one Friday night a man entered the church. He went through the front doors of the little rented building without getting out of his car, at about 100 kph! Not only did he wreck the front of the building, he killed a pedestrian on the steps. This made the building taboo to the Japanese.

Then an insignificant event ushered in a change. While having my hair cut the barber asked me if I played soccer (which I did). When asked if I could referee a game for the local schoolboys on a Saturday afternoon I declined, saying I was too busy. But the Lord spoke to me and I returned to tell the barber I would be available. How could soccer have anything to do with church planting?

Continued

I became something of a local celebrity! People would pass by and see a white-haired foreigner, whistle in his mouth, running around shouting instructions to a crowd of Japanese schoolboys. People made detours on Saturday afternoons to steal a glimpse of this unusual sight. On hot summer afternoons parents brought cool drinks for the coach. On freezing winter afternoons mothers plied me with hot soup. Sarah and I were invited to the sports club picnics and outings where we met many of the parents. I came to know many parents in a very short time. People would stop me on the street and thank me for befriending their children.

In this way some of the suspicion, indifference and resistance towards the Christian fellowship was dispelled. A few boys, and even one or two of the parents, began to attend the meetings at Ishiyama. Not only so, I could now visit a good number of homes as someone more than a complete stranger.

Becoming the football coach gave me a recognisable role in local society, presented me with the opportunity to exercise a spiritual gift, opened the door for spontaneous personal witness, and enhanced the credibility of the local Christian fellowship.

Another insignificant event ushered in an even greater opportunity for evangelism. I was asked to speak to a group of ladies at another WEC Church. The subject given was 'Bringing up children'. (Sarah and I have three girls). Having agreed to speak at the Ladies' Fellowship, I prepared a Bible study-cum-lecture on the Christian home. I included the relationship between husband and wife, and the relationship between parent and child. I illustrated the talk with poems from the Japanese literature I was studying and with many practical examples from our own family life. I concluded the talk with a short testimony of my conversion while a teenager.

About fifteen ladies attended the meeting. Some were not members of the church and had only come because they had been attracted by the subject. After the talk, which lasted about an hour, one of the ladies, who was not a church member, rose. 'Pastor, would you be willing to return to this town in two months time to give this same talk at our annual PTA (Parents and Teachers Association) meeting?' I told her I would do so if she thought it would be helpful. Two months later I returned to the town and made my way to the secondary school. The headmaster escorted me to the sports auditorium. The place was packed. There were about 600 present! At the end of the lecture the audience gave me a spontaneous round of applause.

I knew that in all probability a missionary had never given a lecture at the PTA meeting there before. The Japanese pastors in our fellowship were delighted that a Christian had been given such an opportunity. I went home relieved that the lecture had gone so well. Imagine my surprise when, within two weeks, I had an invitation to speak at another secondary school less than ten miles from Ishiyama.

Continued

It was a very hot day in August. I was met by the PTA president and driven to the school. After exchanging greetings with the school officials and the mayor of the town, I was led to the school auditorium. Over 1,300 parents and teachers were present.

I then received invitations to lecture at ladies' study groups, cultural study groups, Teachers' Trade Union seminars, Rotary clubs and other churches. I was even invited to speak for ninety minutes at the Shiga County Hall to the headmasters of all the primary and secondary schools in the county.

I received letters and phone calls from isolated Christians who were encouraged that a Christian had been asked to speak at such public lectures. Some testified that they had found it much easier to speak about Christ to their friends and relatives after the lecture had taken place. I sometimes received letters from non-Christians who wrote to tell me that their lives had been challenged. The Lord opened a door of opportunity for widespread witness through which He was encouraging scattered Christians throughout Shiga county and through which He was building His church in Ishiyama.

Of all the opportunities I have ever had in Japan this one in particular confirmed to me the value of continuing a systematic study of Japanese language and literature. I would never have been able to speak to such large crowds so often, or to city officials and headmasters with such freedom, if I had not continued to study Japanese even into my third term. Years of hard work were bearing fruit.

Coaching the local boys' football club and lecturing all over the county gave our little family wide and sincere acceptance within the local community of Ishiyama. We were no longer on the outside seeking a way in. We were, to some degree, on the inside with many opportunities to meet people and witness to them.

As the fellowship began to grow, another little shop we had started to use as our meeting place became inadequate for our needs. It could no longer accommodate those who gathered. The growing congregation meant it could now afford to rent more suitable premises.

4

Pass the Baton

Stewart Dinnen

Core Value: *To inspire, mobilise and train
for cross-cultural mission.*

If a man joins our mission, he comes out on God. God is his father, to God
he looks for his supplies whether in money or kind. If God sends much, he
is rather cast down thinking God is afraid to trust him to suffer. If God sends
little, he thanks Him and takes courage that, after all, he may be in the
apostolic succession. If he has nothing, then he shouts hallelujah, for he
knows he has come to the very entrance of the heavenly kingdom where
there is neither eating nor drinking, but righteousness, peace and joy ...

If people want pretty houses and elegant furnishings, for God's sake and
ours, let them stay at home in the nursery.

So wrote C.T. Studd, WEC's founder, from Congo. What a recipe for
recruitment! His concern was that those joining WEC must face the cost and
know their call and respond resolutely to the appeal of Jesus.

Recruitment in WEC has almost always followed personal contact with a
WECer. A life touched by God fires others too ...

Jim and Judy Raymo, former Directors of WEC in USA, came to England in
the early 1970s as part of a team of American university students involved in
tent-making projects and evangelism. For most of the year, the team rented a
large warehouse at Bulstrode (the UK base of WEC) in which to live and work.

Jim recalls:

Along came the annual WEC Open Day, and we had to move out of the
warehouse for several weeks beforehand as the hall had to be set up for the
meetings. Len Moules, then WEC's International Secretary, said to us, 'Why
don't you come and use my office?' As I typed away in Len's office, I came
to enjoy him as an encouraging, kind, witty 'uncle'. I did not realise, at the
time, the burdens he bore for hundreds of WECers around the world, or his
exhausting travel schedule, or his status in the world mission community. He
and his wife, Iris, welcomed us rather wild young Americans as family, never
making us feel that we were taking up their valuable time. From them we
caught a sense of the big-heartedness of WEC, of its desire to be on the

cutting edge of what the Lord is doing, and not to become a tradition-bound organisation – 'another waterlogged craft'. Their lives illuminated to us what C.T. Studd wrote as the basis for the mission's existence:

> Believing that further delay would be sinful, some of God's insignificants, nobodies in particular, conscious of our own impotence and ignorance, but trusting in our Omnipotent God to bring it to pass according to His Word, have decided on certain simple lines, according to the book of God, to make a definite attempt to render the evangelisation of the whole world an accomplished fact.

We've been told that today's young people react negatively to words like 'sacrifice' and are unable or unwilling to make long-term commitments. We've heard that today, decades after C.T. Studd sailed for the heart of Africa, it isn't effective (or maybe even polite!) to say the kinds of things he said to the Christians of his era. We challenge that assumption.

Should we make it easy?

Should our message be different today, somehow made more palatable, more comfortable? From what we've seen in our experience, we would say a resounding NO. God still uses the hot coals of those who have served throughout WEC history to stir people to act and to obey God's call to risk all for the gospel, as these examples illustrate:

> Grace grew up in Korea, served in a church there, but then moved to the USA when her family emigrated. Her English was quite poor, but she knew God was calling her and was determined to complete the WEC Candidate Orientation Course. Despite her natural shyness and desire to make no mistakes, and despite our uncertainty that she would make adequate progress, she spent an entire year in our headquarters working diligently at speaking English and at fitting into our different culture. Her eventual acceptance night was particularly moving for us and for her, as we knew the difficulties she had already overcome. She had the determination and stickability that will serve her well on a tough field.

> John was a pastor of a large Baptist church in California. He was a 'young rising star' in his denomination. Through personal contacts, he visited Spain and our WEC USA headquarters, met a number of missionaries, and collected some literature. He has now resigned from his prestigious, well-paid denominational post and, with his young family, has moved to an area with a very low percentage of Christians to begin a church-planting work.

> At age fourteen, José was a member of a violent street gang in Los Angeles. After seeing his closest friend killed, he came to the Lord. While attending Bible school, he learned that there are groups of pygmy people in Africa who have never heard of Jesus and sensed that the Lord was calling him to help

reach them. José's zeal and single-minded commitment challenged many of us. Although he has ruffled the feathers of some established missionaries, José and his wife are now in Equatorial Guinea and have begun visiting pygmy villages.

Christian workers need to be 'bloodied under combat', and experience active church involvement and evangelistic outreach. We can't afford to send those who have no idea of the battles involved to the tough corners of the world.

Thorough preparation is essential

Anyone wishing to join WEC is required to complete adequate Bible college training. As well as taking people from a huge variety of institutions, the mission has set up its own Missionary Training Colleges in Brazil, Canada, New Zealand, Hong Kong, Australia and the Netherlands. Born out of years of experience, these centres have developed programmes specifically designed for the kind of real life situations that we know exist. Hundreds of graduates are serving with many missionary organisations around the world. WEC takes training very seriously.

Some have called the Candidate Orientation Course 'WEC's secret weapon'. Four months of residential exposure to the mission ethos allows potential missionaries to judge for themselves whether they want to join us. At the same time staff members get to know the candidates well and assess their suitability for their target field. Lectures, prayer, fellowship, practical involvement in the life of the WEC base and prescribed projects help prepare the future missionary.

Sharing the burden wider

As well as recruiting and training, God has enabled WEC to be a catalyst and support in the development of other groups. Leslie Brierley, former International Director for Research, was burdened for WEC to become a mobiliser which would fire others into mission. So he promoted the idea of Centres of Fellowship and Outreach where information could be shared with local Christians about the needs of the unevangelised around the world and assistance offered in getting local organisations up and running.

As well as pushing and publishing his *Look* and *Wider Look* bulletins, Leslie went to Brazil where he fed his ideas into the emerging church. Bob and Bev Harvey took over from his initial efforts and for years toured the country, encouraging the fledgling mission movement. Today there are many Brazilians in cross-cultural ministries.

Work was also done in promoting the worldwide burden in Indonesia, Taiwan, Hong Kong, Singapore, Korea and Nigeria. Various organisations sprang to life and God has greatly blessed these brother agencies.

If we can't go everywhere, we can pass on what little knowledge and expertise we have gained. It is, as Leslie Brierley has said, 'The whole church taking the whole gospel to the whole world.'

Holes in their socks

Rollie Grenier

By the grace of God my wife and I were saved in Lethbridge, Alberta, through the witness and personal testimony of my brother, John (presently a WEC missionary in The Gambia). Only months after our conversion, we could no longer see the sense of continuing with our regular jobs and lifestyle when we knew that millions around the world were dying without knowing the Saviour, so we began a two year ministry in the inner city of Winnipeg, Manitoba, among both the abused and abusers of drugs, alcohol and sex.

Our pastor continued to challenge us and confirm our call to ministry and missions. During our time at Winnipeg Bible College, mission conferences brought us into contact with workers who could answer our questions. As they kicked off their shoes and joined us in our living room, I came to see that WEC missionaries were different. They had holes in their socks! I liked that because, as a student, so did I! They didn't have fancy suits or cars or even big elaborate display tables and brochures, but they had a special 'trust and obey' quality about them that attracted me. Many of them helped and guided us as we sought to discover God's place for us. In all of our times together, I never sensed that they were specifically trying to recruit us for WEC but rather helping us find the Lord's will.

Through a long and prayerful time of searching, we felt that the Lord was leading us to work with WEC reaching Spaniards for Christ. (We are a Spanish-speaking family.)

Prior to finishing Bible school, we had the privilege of meeting Wilf Watson, an older WECer, who had spent thirty years in South America. He was a man we wanted to be like, a man of deep commitment to God and with a burning fire to complete the task of evangelising the world.

Wilf was the first one to introduce us to the little known Spanish-speaking African country of Equatorial Guinea, and to challenge us to pray about going there. Despite the great need, we couldn't imagine ourselves (at least my wife couldn't) going to Africa. Wilf encouraged us to go to Spain but we kept our hearts open to Equatorial Guinea. Wilf's example of sacrificial giving, continuous prayer and spiritual insight made him a spiritual father to us.

The Lord took us to Spain, and just as we were settling in He brought Equatorial Guinea before us again. We heard that the small team of five missionaries who had reopened the field after it had been closed for twenty-three years by the Marxist government, was now down to one couple, and they were leaving soon.

Continued

During the Spanish field conference, Elliott Tepper, the founder of the Betel work, said to me, 'We can't let Satan have the victory in this. Someone must go.'

We prayed, 'Lord, if I could just go and visit the work there, we could pray more intelligently.' We thought that this was a safe prayer as our finances were so low! Then we received a call from Ron Brynjolfson, the outgoing field leader of Equatorial Guinea at the time, who wanted to let us know that someone had designated funds for a survey trip. So the Lord opened the door for me to pay a visit to Equatorial Guinea, right in the middle of government elections and of divisions in the national church. The situation was so complex and desperate that after two weeks I felt sure that God was reconfirming our call to Spain. I couldn't imagine He would send us there as a family.

Back in Spain, I shared the situation with Cristina. She looked me in the eye and said, 'If it is because you are afraid, that's not good enough.' We set a prayer goal for the end of the month, trusting the Lord to guide.

One weekend, near the end of that time, I couldn't sleep. I got up to pray and read my Bible. Not wanting to waken Cristina, I went into the office and turned on the light. On the desk in front of me was C.T. Studd's little book *The Chocolate Soldier*. I sat on the floor and began to read it. As I learned about the heroes of faith, tears came to my eyes. I yearned to be a man of faith and courage for the God who had saved me through the death of His only Son, Jesus. As I dried my eyes, I read the final page of the booklet. It said, 'To your knees, man! And to your Bible. Decide at once! Don't hedge! Time flies! Cease your insults to God. Quit consulting flesh and blood. Stop your lame lying and cowardly excuses. Enlist!'

The end of the month came and the Lord gave us the peace we sought and on top of that He gave us such a joy in knowing and responding to His will. Hallelujah!

We now work in Equatorial Guinea and have the privilege of training young men and women there in the Word of God in order to win Equatorial Guinea for Christ.

5

Jesus Christ Running Around in the Messengers

Neil Rowe

Core Value: *We fervently desire to see Christ formed in us so that we live holy lives.*

Neil Rowe has been a member of the staff at WEC's former Missionary Training College in Scotland, manager of the WEC Press and of Bulstrode, British Director and Regional Director in Africa and the Middle East. His testimony illustrates the truth that WECers have to be people who not only give a mental assent to the doctrine of holiness but really know the truth in their lives. It must actually work in a daily experience of release from sinful bondages and an awareness of God's power moving through all we do so that people we disciple are filled with the same.

Possess your possessions!

I had long accepted the truth expressed in Colossians 1:27 of 'Christ in you, the hope of glory', but somehow I could not get there in terms of my own experience. During one specific period of earnest seeking, as I travelled in Africa, I marked every reference in the New Testament that implied union with Christ. Steadily the margins of my *Revised Standard Version* filled up with 'U' for stated union or 'IU' for implied union. Later, I realised that the translators of the *Good News Bible* (GNB) had set out from the beginning to express 'our being in Christ' or 'Christ being in us' as union, so Bible quotations in this chapter are from the GNB unless otherwise stated.

Another very meaningful quotation that found its way on to the flyleaf of that Bible was from a book by Norman Grubb called *Who Am I?* It said:

My need therefore is not to have more, but to possess my possessions. To know who I am, not who I ought to become. Not to acquire, but to recognise.

I knew that there was a real significance for me in these words, though I couldn't grasp it there and then because I didn't understand the full significance of union with Christ.

Many of us have been challenged by the deep desire of C.T. Studd, in the founding days of the work, to 'see Jesus running about in black bodies'. If we accept his vision, then we must also accept that it can legitimately be turned

round and become a pointed question – How can that happen, except they see
Jesus Christ running around in the messengers?

We are all different, and I have to confess to being more impressed by the life
of Studd's biographer, Norman Grubb, than with Studd himself. Although I am
but one of hundreds, probably thousands, called by God through that biography,
I am even more deeply touched by what Norman Grubb achieved. Following the
death of Studd in 1931, Norman Grubb rebuilt the mission which was virtually
in ruins. It was the worst possible time, at the height of the depression in Britain.
The task facing him was to resurrect, rebuild, and strengthen the mission, which
God enabled him to do in incredible ways, not least through his ability to grasp
and apply spiritual truth to real life situations. He dealt with the twin themes of
Holiness and Union with Christ, and showed us that true holiness can only flow
out of the life of the Holy One.

So how does this come about?

The way through

In Romans 6:6 Paul says: 'And we know that our old being has been put to death
with Christ on his cross, in order that the power of the sinful self might be
destroyed ... so that we should no longer be the slaves of sin.' This is not
salvation, dealing with past sin through Christ dying for us; but our dying **with**
Him, thus dealing with our old nature. And the purpose is crystal clear – that we
should no longer be the slaves of sin.

Many struggle with 'dying to self', and this problem hinders us from
appropriating fully the truth of Colossians 1:27 – 'Christ in you the hope of
glory.' Who is going to stand up and say 'Christ lives in me' when they know
they live a defeated life, when they know that sin and self are still very much
alive in spite of a salvation testimony? Many somehow believe that death means
an annihilation or eradication of the old nature, but they find they cannot achieve
that position. No wonder!

As it is used here in Romans 'death' means 'separation from'. As I have died
with Christ, God really sees me as being separated from sin and Satan. It is no
longer I, because that old 'I' has been nailed to the cross with Christ. Now the
new redeemed me has a totally new God-orientation instead of the old
sin/self/Satan-orientation.

We must realise that God is not asking us to put ourselves to death. Just the
opposite. He wants to bring the real you to life – free from the control of sin and
Satan, and able to manifest the fruits of the Spirit instead of the fruits of the
flesh. Paul does not simply say 'not I but Christ' – he says 'not I but Christ *lives
in me.*' The 'me' is there, but not the self under Satan's domination. The true
'me' now comes to life in His resurrection life. Romans 6:6 also helps to clarify
this when Paul says: 'And we know that our old being has been put to death with
Christ on his cross, in order that the **power** of the sinful self might be destroyed
... so that we should no longer be the slaves of sin.' It is not the self – the special

person that God has made you – that is the problem, but the corrupted self that Satan has hijacked you into becoming. Dying with Christ, dying to self, means just what Paul says – the **power** of the sinful self-being destroyed. Strong language!

For any who have difficulty over the concept of union, I want to add a quote from a magazine article written by Stewart Dinnen on this topic. He says: 'What helped me to see this was the fact that in Romans 6 all the Greek verbs used have the prefix *sun*, meaning "together with": *sunthapto* (v.4) – "buried (together) with"; *sumphuo* (v.5) – "united (together) with"; *sustauroo* (v.6) – "crucified (together) with"; *sunzao* (v.8) – "live (together) with".'

Clay pots

Paul uses a very helpful illustration in 2 Corinthians 4, when he says that we are like clay pots – common or ordinary ones at that. To digress a moment, I find that many believers, including Christian workers, are really unable to accept themselves. Certainly I was like that, though I would not admit it openly. I looked at others and wished I could preach like him, teach like her, think quickly, have a more dynamic personality, be more gifted in this or that area. Basically it was a non-acceptance of the kind of 'pot' that God had made me.

Then, as part of the package that came with recognising Christ in me, I realised that I have a 'made in' stamp at the bottom of my mug, or whatever shape vessel God has made me. He knew me before I was born, even before I was conceived. He knew my background, my inherited weaknesses, my inabilities and all the rest. Suddenly I found that I could accept myself because He accepted me enough to live in me! The shape and purpose of the clay pot did not matter – fit for the table of a king, or just to hold the salt in the kitchen! What mattered was that first the clay pot was scrubbed clean (cleansed by the blood of Christ) then filled with treasure (Christ Himself). Such recognition brings incredible relief. No longer did I have to pretend, or try to be someone I was not meant to be. 'Relax' suddenly became a key word to me because I had always been ruled by inner tension. Circumstances of heredity, upbringing, and all the rest no longer remain negative factors, always pulling us down, but, incredibly, as part of His master design, they become positive as we are pleased to be what He planned us to be, in our union with Him! Wonderful!

Recognising that Christ lives in you brings a new dimension to daily living. Before, when something happened to me, and I needed help, I would have to pray to Christ 'out there' or 'up there'. I would need to explain to Him exactly what had happened. But now, things don't just happen to me, they happen to Christ in me. He knows before I need to tell Him.

A ladleful of love

Before, when I would run up against some difficult character, I would cry to God to help me, usually to give me more love. Norman Grubb uses such a simple illustration that I can't better it. He says that most of us see God/Christ sitting up there in heaven with a huge bowl labelled 'LOVE'. When we cry out loud enough or plead our case strongly enough He will pass us down a ladleful.

The truth is that God does not HAVE love – He IS love! It is not a commodity for stocking on the shelf until needed. When we recognise Christ in us, we recognise His love in us. Instead of having to screw ourselves up in order to try and show extra love towards that difficult person, we relax, die to ourselves (i.e. our selfish desire to justify, get equal, outdo or whatever) and allow Him to love that person through us.

Love is but one attribute available to us. Other scriptures have a new freshness when viewed from the standpoint of a union relationship: 'My strength is made perfect in weakness' for example.

I always felt so inadequate. I knew my own family background; I knew my own lack of higher education; I knew my own weaknesses and failures. I felt so inadequate but I didn't let on. That would never do! A sign of weakness! So I struggled inwardly, very often being propped up by my wife, Mary. My encounter with God in recognising my union relationship with Him through Christ was revolutionary. Now I happily admit to being inadequate. That's no problem because I have the 'Adequate One' within. I can't – but He can. What a relief! No wonder that some weeks after my experience, Mary told others that she had a new husband.

Some will rightly ask if this has to be a second, after conversion, experience. The answer is no – but it generally is. The simple fact is that few of us are sufficiently well taught at conversion to take in the whole new living landscape that is presented to us.

There is nothing to hinder any of us understanding, recognising and appropriating this truth of Christ in us at conversion. In practice it seems that many come to it through a gradual dawning of spiritual truth, and move into a position of recognising truth and exercising faith in spiritual fact.

So in WEC we believe that irrespective of a person's Christian background, there must be an understanding of who we are, of what Jesus has done for us, and how we experience freedom from sin and unnecessary personal baggage. The life of Jesus through the indwelling Spirit must become an integral part of our lives so that we can serve with freedom and power. To touch the world God must move in and through the messenger.

The veneer was wearing thin ...

Neil Rowe

It was after twenty years in Christian ministry that God cornered me. I was on a two-month tour of Africa at the time. As I moved from country to country, the demands seemed to increase. Fellow workers expected me to have the answers to their problems, to be able to preach and teach at the drop of a hat, to counsel, advise, guide, and all the rest. I became more and more tense, and more and more angry at God because He was always stretching me – asking more of me than I could give. My spiritual veneer was wearing very thin, and the inadequacies were showing through!

The final country of the tour was Congo. At the time, I had been reading and rereading *Who Am I?* by Norman Grubb and these words had grabbed me:

My need therefore is not to have more, but to possess my possessions.
To know who I am, not who I ought to become. Not to acquire, but to recognise.

I kept reading because I told myself that there was something that I was missing; in fact that wasn't the case. I was simply failing to believe, in the sense of exercising biblical faith, and failing to stand upon a truth as if it were a solid bridge over a deep chasm. My visit was nearly up and I was due to leave on the Saturday, flying by MAF plane to Kenya and then by regular airline to Britain. I had heard the Africans talk about their huge evangelistic conferences – maybe up to 5,000 people at a time. I commented that I was sorry that I had not seen one. The truth was that I really wanted some good photos for a magazine article and some good slides to show at home! Then there was trouble over the border in Uganda. Its airspace was closed and my MAF flight was cancelled for at least a week. In the light of this the church leaders said that they would now organise a conference for me!

I was in my element as they cleared a huge area like a football stadium. Within four days it was looking great, and I had some excellent photos. Only then did I casually ask one of the pastors which of them would be preaching. He immediately replied, 'You, of course.' That was terrible! I went to my room to have it out with God. I was angry inside. 'This is the same old story,' I told Him. 'You are always stretching me. Always asking more of me than I am able to give. I'm not an evangelist. I don't have that gift. I don't know these people. I don't know their language. I don't know their culture.' So I went on and on. Deep down, of course, I knew that my biggest fear was of making an appeal at the end and seeing no-one respond. I had often heard of the large numbers who came to Christ at these gatherings, but I could see a different day dawning – one of zero response! It was pure pride, of course – another evidence that I had not effectively died to my old nature.

Next morning I turned to my regular reading, and started at 2 Corinthians 5. I came to verse 20, which reads in the RSV, 'So we are ambassadors for God, God

Continued

making his appeal through us.' That broke me. It was as if God said to me, 'I'll do the work – I just want your co-operation. You die – and I'll live through you.' That evening I took a deliberate step of faith. I told my Lord that I would recognise the truth of scripture, that I would give Him His rightful place, that I would die to my old self (in which Satan had been my illegitimate intruder/slave-master), that I would stand on this wonderful truth of Christ in me, that it did not matter to me (my pride) what happened at the appeal on Saturday. With that I relaxed and slept. When Saturday came, I was totally at ease. Yes, I had done my homework in preparation. (Christ in us can never be an excuse for not acting responsibly and for doing what we should do.) When I made the appeal, large numbers came forward. It was only afterwards that I learned the reason. While some of the men were preparing the site, other men and women from the church were out evangelising in the surrounding villages, inviting people to the conference. Many, in fact, had already decided to follow Christ, but had been told to go forward at the appeal for proper counselling!

That made no real difference. I had proved God. He had met me. Life changed from that point. My only regret is that I struggled for so long, overlooking the truth of scripture, and missing so much in terms of richness. Who cares what shape of pot I am, or what I look like, or what my history is – it is the Resident Treasure that matters.

Death to self became a reality in daily living. I knew release from anger, inner frustration, jealousy, pride and all the rest. Not 'perfection' in the sense of sinlessness, I hasten to add, but growing 'maturity in union with Christ' as Paul set out to achieve. Not self effort – thank God. Not I – but Christ in me – thank God again!

Slowly it dawned on me that this was holiness – Christ living His holy life in me. Not my seeking to achieve a standard defined by man, but allowing Him to be what He is – in me and through me. I Corinthians 1:30-31 sums it up: 'But God has brought you into union with Christ Jesus ... by Him we are put right with God, we become God's holy people and are set free.'

A statement by Stewart Dinnen found its way on to the flyleaf of my Bible because it says so concisely what I am proving in daily life: 'Holiness – through realised union with Christ in His death and resurrection.' The stress has to be on 'realised'. The actual truth stands, of course, whether you acknowledge it or not. But it only becomes real as we recognise it, realise it, appropriate it, stand firm on it and make it part of our daily living.

In closing let me quote from C.S. Lewis in *Mere Christianity*:

> Some think that to become a new person means losing what we now call 'ourselves'. The truth is that the more we get what we now call 'ourselves' out of the way and let Him take over, the more ourselves we become.

6

A Costly Business

Evan Davies

Core Value: *In dependence on the Holy Spirit we determine to obey the Lord whatever the cost.*

It's no joke

Being a Christian servant is no joke. It is serious business and we are warned by Jesus that carrying our cross is part of discipleship (Luke 14:26-27). Here are two stories to illustrate this:

> I was called over in front of one of the policemen. He had one of our hymnbooks in his hands and asked me for an explanation of the notes. I gave him this. He asked me to sing a hymn to them, adding that he would choose the one to sing. Of all the hymns in the book, the one he chose was 'Take my life, and let it be consecrated, Lord, to Thee'. After I had sung he put his foot behind me, and with his fist knocked me to the ground. This was repeated three times. Hymn, blow! Hymn, blow! Hymn, blow! And once more we were ordered into the tank of water and out of it again to more running around.
> (W.C. Easton, *Colombian Conflict,* 1954, Christian Literature Crusade, London)

> The minibus climbed to the top (of the mountain pass) and in descending, John got behind a convoy of army vehicles carrying rice. Suddenly gunfire, the shouts of men; the Viet Cong had attacked! A bullet whipped into the side of the minibus. John was killed outright in a flash. When, a little later, American missionaries arrived on the scene, his body was found in a metal culvert running under the road. Death had come suddenly to one who, during his short missionary career, had written, 'I am not here for thrills. I have a job to do, and I can best do it while I am alive. There are just not enough hours in the day for the work I have in hand.'

> (B. Macindoe, *Only One Life*, 1966, WEC Press, Gerrards Cross, Bucks.)

Study the lives of those who are part of God's apostolic band (missionaries) and you find difficulties, persecution and, in some cases, death. No greater tribute can be given than that said of Paul and Silas in Acts 15:26: 'Men who have risked their lives for the name of our Lord Jesus Christ.' Christian workers today have no cause to think they will escape hardship in fulfilling their calling. In many of the places to which they go political tensions are barely below the surface and national secular leadership, with a pride in its independence, is not afraid to humiliate or ignore foreigners. Christianity is often not welcome and, in many cases, the church is not of significant size in the community. In addition, there is a rising tide of anti-Christian religious intolerance, which is resulting in harassment of Christians, opposition to institutional Christianity and hostility to missionaries.

Tough going

The Christian missionary knowingly faces a whole range of costly choices. To start with, there is the spiritual cost arising from living in a new environment away from home church, pastoral care, and long-standing Christian friends. Uprooted from the familiar and plunged into a new setting, the worker faces the temptation to succumb to overwork, to lower moral defences and to lose the sharp edge of spirituality because of self-interest or lack of realistic contact with God. Even in the area of forgiveness, the missionary can let personal reactions replace love for our enemies. Cathy Church writes:

> Compare my small amount of suffering with the suffering of the Sri Lankan Christians. I mean, I lost everything I owned. But how much was that worth? Maybe $500, if you take all my suitcases, my clothes, my radio. And yet people lost their whole life-savings. The majority of Christians lost everything.

> And then you have the Christians who watched their spouses die. Others were raped. In that context, my suffering was small. Yet I could see from the little things I suffered, how much hatred and anger and unforgiveness was in my heart.

> (Glenn Myers, *Learning to Forgive: Cathy's Story*, 1997, Christian Focus Publications, Scotland.)

Then there is the cost to health. We are familiar with the scenario in the tropical world of bugs, parasites, diseases and resistant strains of malaria. In many countries there are inadequate health services – doctors are far apart and medicines in short supply; there are few ambulances or adequately supplied clinics and hospitals; hygiene is not a high priority and many staff have not had first-rate training. The HIV/AIDS pandemic and outbreaks like SARS make medical treatment dangerous to both patient and medical staff. In other places the cost of good health care is prohibitive. The story of missionary work contains many instances of those who suffered in health and in some cases died as a result.

The costs to the family have to be faced. Consider parents contemplating taking their children to a new country. The schooling may be different, inadequate or non-existent. How can children eventually reintegrate into highly competitive societies? What of health issues? The loss of personal space? The deprivation of close friends, home comforts, regular family visits and church environment? The heartache of being separated from family who go to boarding school is a daunting prospect for parents and children – even though in most cases the whole experience is wonderfully fulfilling. Whatever we may think of Jesus' remarkable words in Matthew 19:29: 'And every one who has left houses or brothers or sisters or father or mother or children or fields for my sake will receive a hundred times as much and will inherit eternal life', there is a cost in leaving family but there are glorious rewards. To obey the supreme commands of Jesus, tough family decisions have to be made.

Then there is the cost of adapting to another culture. New country, new language, new customs and a whole new educational structure in the adopted society force the missionary into totally unfamiliar territory. With whom are they going to identify – with his or her own colleagues, the home culture or the local culture? Strange customs may tempt the missionary to withdraw and resist exposure and identification while others shy away from learning the language well and plunge into activity. They forget that culture and language are the keys to long-term involvement and heart identification.

Civil war takes its toll

The political cost is often the most obvious. Missionaries may be caught up in civil war or hostilities between opposing countries. In the fierce days accompanying the birth of India and Pakistan, the WEC team in Kashmir was caught up in terrifying events. While most managed to get to safety, Ron Davies, a former communist who was then field leader, stayed to be with, and hopefully protect, two local Christians. One of them, Miriam, asked by the invading Pathans to deny Christ and revert to Islam, refused and was shot. It seems that in a very few minutes Ron followed her.

Buffeted savagely, he was asked who he was and if he was ready to die. He said that he was Ronald Davies, Khadim Masik ('Servant of Christ' – his self-chosen name), and that he was ready. Once more the rifles cracked and Ron died beside Miriam. Wild wanton debauchery continued.

(J. Purves *Lal Sahib: The Story of Ronald Davies,* 1950, Stirling Tract Enterprises, Scotland.)

In the chaotic days following the granting of independence by the Belgians to the Congo, WEC missionaries were caught up in the civil war and in the attempts to turn the northeastern area back to pre-Christian days. It was a terrible time. Beatings, rape and killings were the order of the day. Foreigners and African leaders alike were badly treated. WEC lost five missionaries. It is recorded that:

During Wednesday morning a mortar shell exploded outside the missionary prison killing ten rebels. Immediately the guard saw his fellows killed, he took a machete and attacked, severely wounding Mrs Taylor and her two little girls. The family was taken down to the low-level dungeon-like room where Muriel (Harman) and the nuns attended to the wounds with handkerchiefs. They could do very little, for surgical stitching of the terrible gaping wound was needed.

Desperate for reprisal the rebels ordered all out of the cells up to another room. The wounded could not move. Muriel tried to tend them but was ordered above. They filed into a long room. Men were backed to the wall on one side, and women against the other. Automatic weapons were loaded and the rebels marched down each line pouring a hail of lead into each prisoner. Cyril Taylor was first and, with Muriel, was with the Lord immediately. (L.C. Moules, *This is No Accident*, 1965, WEC International, UK.)

A price to pay

What has happened to WEC missionaries is not unusual in missionary history. There have been many martyrs. Even today evacuations from various countries are common. Sometimes God's servants are harassed by suspicious police and governments. Time in jail is not uncommon; false accusations are made; kidnappings still happen. To distribute the Bible or to initiate a conversation about Christianity carries the threat of immediate expulsion. The isolation, ostracism or severe persecution faced by converts are daunting.

After the tragic experience of losing their teenage son, Josue, in Equatorial Guinea, Cristina Grenier said:

In WEC we need people who are going to go in and stay in, despite isolation, sickness, despair, failure, many things. We have to be out there, willing to stay, year after year until we see completion. I also think when we are recruiting, we need to tell people there is a cost. If you are willing to serve, you have to be willing to sacrifice. There is a price tag attached to our airline ticket, a tag of sacrifice. (*Renewed to Run for Jesus*: Devotional material for Intercon 2002, WEC International).

Yet it is wrong to portray missionary work as all dread and gloom. Not all lose their lives, suffer severe illnesses, face vicious hostility or go through deeply traumatic experiences. For most, missionary work is deeply satisfying, often bringing the highest fulfilment in a life devoted to service. Cross-cultural friendships are formed, the culture and food(!) of the target country become a delightful part of life, and, afterwards, long years of ministry are treasured with nostalgia.

Still it is important to count the cost. Remember what Jesus said in Luke 14:28-33? Don't rush in without weighing things up in advance. Am I willing to put aside possessions, personal safety, comfort and anything else that will jeopardise the fulfilling of the heavenly mandate? In Acts 20:22-24 Paul says: 'I consider my life worth nothing to me, if only I may finish the race and complete the task the Lord Jesus has given me – the task of testifying to the gospel of God's grace'; and in Philippians 3:7-14: 'I consider everything a loss compared to the surpassing greatness of knowing Christ Jesus my Lord.'

Life is irrelevant unless Jesus is central and accomplishing His objectives through us. This is, in fact, the prime objective for all, whether ordinary Christian, church leader or missionary.

For no one else but you, Lord

Susan Sutton

As part of the cost of reaching the unreached in Chad, American WECer Susan Sutton faces frequent separation from her son and twin daughters. On one occasion she wrote:

I woke up this morning thinking, 'I don't want to be at this point. Not at the end of vacation. Not at the time to say goodbye – again.'

We have just spent a wonderful two weeks as a family; a cherished time of non-stop togetherness, laughter, hugs and discussion. And today it ends for another three months. We will send the children back to boarding school and Louis and I will head back to a house that seems too quiet, too empty, after all the energy that has just left.

Saying goodbye does not become easy just because we have done it before. Separation from our children so they can receive a good education while we continue our ministry is the hardest thing God has asked of us yet. Sometimes, the ache of missing them is so great I have to say to the Lord, 'I wouldn't do this for anyone else but You.'

And that is true. Only the Lord is worthy of such a sacrifice. I do not think He asks it of us lightly. He knows full well what such a sacrifice means.

Jesus knew what it is like to be asked to do a hard thing, something He would have preferred not to experience. (Thank You, Lord, for Your honesty in Gethsemane.) He knew the keenest pain of separation at the cross, when our sin, placed on His shoulders, blocked all access to the One He loved most.

When the Lord made it clear that our work in Chad was not finished and that we should return for a third term, Louis and I knew that our children would need more from school than we could offer at home in a bush town. It was the hardest decision we have ever had to make and the bottom line was trust.

I struggled with the Lord for nearly a year. Surely He had given us children as a responsibility and never meant us to give that responsibility to someone else. My arguments were plenty.

'Yes, Lord, I know that one day they'll need to be on their own, independent from us. But not at twelve and fourteen years old! Never mind that others have done it far earlier and sent their children further away for the sake of the gospel. We're talking about *our* family and what is right for *us*.'

The turning point came one day when I was praying for the children. I was using

Continued

a guide to family prayer, which my mother-in-law had recently sent to me. On this particular day, I was praying the words that followed the question, 'Lord, what do You want for my children?'

The prayer went along these lines:

> I release them to You so You can accomplish Your will for their lives.
> (Pause … hmmmm)

> I will not try to relive my life through them. Keep me from binding them by my needs, wants and ambitions for them.

> (Longer pause, and a growing sense of uneasiness)

> Get me out of Your way, so that You can work the life of Christ in them, and give them your best.

> (Okay, Lord, enough! I surrender.)

I knew at that moment that I was praying one thing, yet working hard for another. By digging in my heels over the issue of separation, I was in danger of working against what God wanted to do in the lives of my children.

From this heavenly perspective, boarding school was not merely a solution to remaining on the field, it was the very thing God wanted for our children. It was the new arena in which He intended to shape their lives. As parents, we had to trust Him in this – that He knew what He was doing with our children.

Letting go was the first and hardest step. Then we simply watched God's faithfulness unfold. How we came to send the children to Black Forest Academy in Germany while we work in Africa is a story in itself. But from the minute the decision was made, we have known it was right. The children love the Academy and we are continually thankful they are in such a good place.

Still, it is not easy to say goodbye again. But it helps when I read a note like the one Liz slipped into my hand, saying, 'Mom, read this when you're on your way home.'

Later I pulled the flowered stationery from its matching envelope:

> Dearest Mom and Dad,

> Last year at the beginning of school, you said, 'I feel as if I am giving away my treasures.'

> Well, I just wanted to remind you, as an encouragement, that for one thing, as a baby, you gave our lives to the Lord, as well as each one of us having at one point given up our own lives again to Him … mind, soul, spirit, body.

> Therefore we are not yours to give! And you know God won't give us up!

> Have a safe trip home.

So, why am I crying? It looks as if God knows what He is doing!

7

Trust God? Absolutely!

Evan Davies

Core Values: *We trust God completely to meet every need and challenge we face in His service. We make no appeals for funds.*

In WEC we can take courage from the promise 'I will never stop doing them good … I will rejoice in doing them good' (Jeremiah 32:40-44). God's promises are positive and generous. His formula for answering joint prayer is evidence of His faithful character. We see this in Matthew 18:19,20 where we read: 'If two of you on earth agree about anything you ask for, it will be done for you by my Father in heaven. For where two or three come together in my name, there am I with them.'

The Bible is full of examples of people of faith. The famous passage in Hebrews 11 gives an Old Testament overview. God was not interested in the theory but in the practice of faith. When people acted on the promises and instruction of God, there was meant to be a result. James tells us: 'Do not merely listen to the word … Do what it says … faith by itself, if it is not accompanied by action, is dead' (James 1:22; 2:17,24).

When we talk about faith in the biblical context, we are talking about a settled trust in God. Faith is based on the great objective facts of Christianity – the character of God, the divinity of Christ, the presence of the Holy Spirit, the inspiration of the Bible and the efficacy of Jesus' death to transform both the worst and best specimens of humanity into children of the living God.

God has encouraged us not to be complacent but to take the initiative in faith. We must be proactive. Jesus rebuked the disciples for their insignificant faith (Matthew 17:20; Luke 12:28) but commended the faith of the Roman centurion (Matthew 8:10), the four friends (Mark 2:5), the woman with the haemorrhage (Luke 8:48), the two blind men (Matthew 9:29), and the Lebanese woman (Matthew 15:28). In fact, Jesus went further and positively urged all His followers to use what little faith they had and to get into the mountain-moving business (Matthew 17:20; Mark 11:22-24)!

The apostles went into their evangelistic service trusting God and seemed reluctant to ask for personal support. They believed that the God they served could meet their every need. After all, this is what Jesus asked of them when He said: 'Do not worry about … food … clothes … but seek first His kingdom and His righteousness and all these things will be given to you as well' (Matthew 6:25-34).

So according to Matthew 18:19-20, John 14:13-14, John 15:7 and John 16: 23-24, it follows that in a modern Christian organisation, personnel, permissions, solutions to intractable problems as well as material needs can all be specifically taken by faith.

What bearing does this biblical principle have on the ethos of WEC? Well, first of all, we call ourselves a faith mission, and, in fact, we are one of a rare breed which does not make direct or indirect appeals for finance. WEC has always had great admiration for George Mueller and Hudson Taylor who had experienced powerful examples of God's care for His children. As Hudson Taylor once said 'God's work done in God's way will never lack God's supply.' To take this position does not imply secrecy about money – audited statements of income are readily available, and we are happy to provide information to enquirers when asked. However, we do not take the initiative in making our needs known but trust God implicitly to make provision for us through whatever channel He pleases to use.

We wholeheartedly appreciate churches and individuals who have a sense of responsibility for workers going to the field, but we affirm strongly that a new worker should not be dependent on a single source. A church may split, an individual's financial situation could change, but the servant of Christ has a commission that must be fulfilled. So while we do not expect new workers to have guaranteed support before going to the field, we do expect them to have a strong sense of conviction in their calling and in God's ability to meet their needs. Yes, God uses supporters to meet the needs of the Christian worker and the worker has to be faithful in accountability and communication, but they have to stand on the scripture that it is God who supplies all their need (Philippians 4:19).

It is important to say that we appreciate other organisations that use different methods and we respect them highly for their commitment and great faithfulness, but God has led us in a different way and we remain committed to this path.

WEC history is replete with exciting ventures in which faith has played a pivotal role.

By faith, even though past their use-by date, C.T. Studd and his invalid wife became father and mother of a worldwide missionary organisation because they considered Him faithful who had made a promise to CT in 1913 while he was on board a ship going to Africa. He wrote to his wife: 'God has spoken to me in a strange fashion and told me that this trip is not just for the Heart of Africa but for the whole unevangelised world.' In faith, Norman Grubb returned from the field and virtually restarted the work from scratch. He took by faith ten new workers and their support in the first year as a celebratory memorial of Studd's life. (Both my parents were in that group.) In subsequent years, he trusted for fifteen, twenty-five and fifty. By faith Bessie Brierley entered Guinea-Bissau to pioneer in a country closed to all evangelical work. By faith Fred Chapman had a vision for free gospel literature and from that came *Bientôt* (French), *Soon*

(English), *Cedo* (Portuguese) and *Upesi* (Swahili). In 1984 WEC worldwide trusted for 800 new workers which resulted in hundreds of new recruits. By faith the staff, board members and students of Cornerstone Centre in the Netherlands trusted God for a large property and the school next door. By faith Byung Kook and Bo In Yoo started a WEC branch in Korea in 1996 and since then have seen nearly 150 people join WEC and many others involved with other organisations.

The key issue in all faith exploits is not 'Do we have the resources?' Rather, it is 'What is God's will on this matter?' The issue revolves round sensitivity, discernment, and faith, not budgets and financial planning. Here is a sequence that is advocated to our teams as they consider taking steps of faith for some advance:

1. Schedule an unhurried time for fellowship together.
2. Take time for worship, relevant Bible study, and waiting before God, seeking to be sensitive to the Holy Spirit and to each other.
3. Share all needed information relative to the issue about which a decision is needed. Do not be daunted by cost, size and problems.
4. Check that the possible outcome is in line with agreed team policies, strategies and objectives.
5. Discuss what factors in the situation could be indications of the Lord's leading.
6. Lay these perceived evidences before the Lord in prayer, asking for the Spirit's confirmation about them.
7. Trust for a consensus to emerge in line with Col.3:15 ('Let the peace of God be the umpire in your hearts').
8. As the plan crystallises, express faith for the resources needed to accomplish it. Take note of the promises of God.
9. At this point the team needs to declare its faith about what God is going to do, and to praise God for this assurance.
10. Take the necessary steps (again by faith) which will start to implement the decision reached.

For further information on this sequence we recommend the reading of Norman Grubb's little book *Touching the Invisible* (Lutterworth, London 1948 and subsequent editions).

Integral to a trust in God according to Philippines 4:19, we have to take into account Philippians 4:11-13, 2 Corinthians 4:7-12 and 6:3-10. God promises to meet our need, not our greed. Self-discipline and sacrifice are to be deliberate choices and a correction to the false notion that God's people should always have the best.

It seems crazy but this faith life works. When we spend time finding out God's will, we can trust Him to meet every need as we work with Him. Today in WEC, hundreds of workers are seeing God provide, month by month, for their daily needs and the tools to accomplish His task to disciple the nations.

Greater than we could ask or imagine

Jeanette Cooke

After many months of looking for a property to house the Euro Missionary Training College (Cornerstone Centre for Intercultural Studies) and after many disappointments, the Lord brought to our attention a suitable property for sale in Beugen. It had been a convent and the sisters were moving out.

In early October 1988 the European WEC leaders, together with Lindsay McKenzie and Ron and Jeanette Cooke, were due to meet in Emmeloord to decide whether or not we should go ahead and purchase this property. The day before that meeting we were informed that the Dutch Government would not grant visas for overseas staff or students. What was the Lord saying?

The meeting took place as scheduled. It was an emotional time, and at the end of the day we were weary and there was still no clear indication of what the Lord was saying. We concluded the meeting and went off individually to seek the Lord.

The following morning we left as a group for Beugen. We spent some hours looking over the property and then met to share with each other what we felt the Lord was saying. I will never forget that meeting. It is impossible to convey the whole story – the atmosphere in the room, the sense of the Lord's presence, the unity. Each individual had a word from the Lord, different thoughts and verses, but the message was very clear. The Lord's word to us, both as individuals and as a Mission was: 'Step out in faith and obedience and take possession of the land (the property) that I, the Lord your God, am giving to you.' Hanging on to His word and His promises, and with half the needed money in hand, we began negotiations to purchase. In an amazing way the sisters at the convent decided to lower the price substantially.

The final payment had to be made by 1 March 1989. Would we make it? What if the money didn't come in? Yes, we must admit that at times our faith wavered. But our God is faithful to His every word. The deadline was met and WEC International became the owner of this lovely property. We were blessed greatly to have a large quantity of furniture, linen and equipment donated for use. Nine months later we were able to welcome the first intake of students and celebrate the opening of the Euro MTC.

8

We're a Family

Linda Chamberlain

Core Value: *We are committed to oneness,*
fellowship, and the care of our whole missionary family.

'That's what I appreciate about WEC. It's like belonging to one big family!' Liz, a missionary candidate nearing the end of her orientation course, was expressing gratitude for the love and care she had received throughout the previous four months. 'It hasn't all been heaven on earth,' she admitted. 'We've rubbed shoulders and had our differences but I feel loved and accepted within the fellowship.' At the close of the course, in true WEC tradition, the leader of the sending base extended to her the right hand of fellowship, a symbolic act of acceptance into the mission.

It hadn't taken Liz long to discover that WEC wasn't perfect. We all need to keep working at fellowship. She had read in the mission handbook, 'Because of our oneness in Him we seek to love and work as people endeavouring to maintain the unity of the Spirit in the bond of peace' (Eph 4:3), but she soon saw that this was not a foregone conclusion. Toes can be stood upon, misunderstandings can arise, but when that happens we seek to implement 1 John 1:7: 'If we walk in the light, as He is in the light, we have fellowship with one another, and the blood of Jesus, His Son, purifies us from all sin.'

Oneness discovered

After the death of C.T. Studd in 1931, a second generation of missionaries emerged under the leadership of Norman Grubb. It was in the 1940s that the fellowship factor came into WEC through the influence of the revival in Rwanda, East Africa. Norman visited a CMS station there and saw for himself what other WEC missionaries had witnessed: 'An open sharing with each other where the Spirit convicted them and the blood of Jesus cleansed them ... A brokenness, a down-to-earth reality about their faith, a fellowship which started in sinnerhood at the foot of the cross, and in honest sharing of the Lord's dealing with each other.' God dealt in a fresh way with Norman and other WEC leaders, revealing hidden spots in their lives and encouraging them to this new openness and oneness in fellowship. A while later, two African Christians visited our London headquarters and they made a great impact upon those present. Of that visit Norman wrote: 'The poise, humility, liberty and faithfulness of these two, with their simple magnifying of Jesus in all they said and did, reached our hearts.'

These encounters resulted in a new era for WEC in which this ingredient called 'fellowship' breathed freshness into our meetings. Norman added, 'In these ways there began among us the habit of a more open sharing of the Lord's dealings in our daily lives; it spread to many of our fields and other home bases.' As time went by Norman recognised that enjoying this oneness of fellowship was one thing, but continually living it out was another! He discovered there was one key factor to maintaining this 'unity of the Spirit in the bond of peace' – a recognition of the simple but profound principle of Christ in us. He wrote:

> Years of experience and experimentation have taught us some workable principles. The basic one is unchangeable and unconquerable. It is the fixed fact of Christ in us. If we believe *that* of ourselves, and thus of our brethren in grace, then the foundation of a preserved unity is unalterable. We do not become one or restore a broken oneness. It cannot be broken. But surface disagreements can be so real that we regard it as broken and act as if it were broken. We allow ourselves to be trapped into the illusion of unbelief. What is on the surface has a more real impact on us than the unchangeable foundation beneath. Being human, we are meant to start with our negative human reactions. That is not wrong, it is natural, so long as they are a springboard for faith and not a cushion to sink back into personal feelings.

Oneness in doubt

Stewart Dinnen, a more recent WEC leader said:

> No spiritual principle is more precious and yet no principle is so fiercely attacked by the enemy, because the devil is aware that our oneness means blessing and advance for the kingdom, whereas disharmony and critical attitudes grieve the sensitive Spirit of God and effectively put a brake on its growth. It is a costly principle; costly to establish because it inevitably means a humiliating break before God and before our fellow workers, and costly to maintain because God requires that we keep short accounts.

Stewart recalls one morning when he argued this principle out with God. He was seeking to prepare a lecture which was due to start within the hour. Thoughts and ideas would not flow.

> 'What's wrong, Lord?'
> 'You spoke brusquely to your secretary half an hour ago. Go and apologise.'
> 'I can't do that Lord. I'm the college Principal!'
> 'No breaking, no blessing; no blessing means no lecture.'

Stewart was cornered and shamefacedly took his apology to his secretary. Back in his office, with the oneness restored, he found that ideas flowed, concepts gelled and the lecture was ready in time.

Today in WEC we are still committed to maintaining this costly 'oneness at the foot of the cross'. Hans Schütze, leader of the Brazilian sending base reports on a recent experience:

We had a remarkable chapel time a short while ago. It was a candidate's turn to preach. He shared some thoughts about unity, oneness and our commitment to one another. God began to speak deeply to our hearts. At that time there were some staff members who had problems among themselves. Conflicts in the past had sown seeds of mistrust. There was lack of love, unresolved issues and unforgiveness but God's Spirit began to operate in a tremendous way. Hidden thoughts and attitudes began to come to light as one by one we shared openly about our problems. There was a lovely atmosphere of sharing, of walking in the light, of asking and receiving forgiveness, prayer and reassuring hugs, and holding hands as a symbol of renewed peace with each other. Four hours passed by, we had forgotten about lunch! This remarkable event helped us to get closer together and really express our desire to live and work in fellowship, not allowing the enemy to interfere and to destroy our oneness.

Oneness demonstrated

Keith and Alison Gibson, teachers at the Bourofaye Christian School in Senegal, tell how love and care were demonstrated to them. Alison writes:

Twelve weeks into a pregnancy I lost my baby. The children and staff around me were marvellous. Within minutes of our loss, their instant prayers buoyed us up. The fellowship clubbed together, giving us enough money to convalesce for a weekend at a beach hotel. We travelled by private car (a real luxury), went sail boarding and ate spit roast lamb. The gift was a practical demonstration of the team's love for us and the time and space it gave my husband and me were just what we needed.

From Spain the WEC field leader, Jaap de Bruine, writes:

We have been blessed in so many ways by the care shown by members of the WEC family. In early 1997 our fifteen-year-old son, Jonnie, was diagnosed as having a brain tumour. Suze and I, though shocked, took some comfort in the doctor's words, 'This kind of tumour is usually benign.' Through the use of the Internet, news spread rapidly throughout the WEC world and words of encouragement flowed back. We don't have the words to express our thanks for so many e-mail letters, phone calls and cards expressing heartfelt concern for Jonnie … We feel so loved and encouraged.

Many friends have taken our burden as if it were their own. Many have shared our information, putting it on prayer chains throughout the world. The result has become a great united and agreeing army interceding for a fifteen-year-old child of God in need.

The family was to experience more of that love later when the doctor shared with them the results of surgery. Jonnie's brain tumour was not benign but aggressively malignant, warranting further treatment. The radiotherapy treatment prescribed by the oncologist was expensive. Friends around them began to identify with this need.

After radiotherapy treatment Jonnie began to make an amazing recovery. Time and again Jaap and Suze accredited his progress to answered prayer. It may be several years before they can be confident that Jonnie is free from cancer cells, but they are confident of God's love and the love of their fellow missionaries. They wrote to their friends:

> Again, from the bottom of our hearts, we want to say a big thank you for the love, care and friendship we have experienced from you these past months. We will never be the same. Apart from God's direct intervention, your input into our lives has contributed to a wider conscious awareness of His worldwide church as a caring body of believers. We feel so overwhelmed and privileged to be members of His family.

Oneness deliberated

This commitment to our oneness, to love and to care, cannot be taken for granted. It is something to be worked at, guarded and constantly nurtured. A team member involved in a ministry within a restricted access nation speaks of ways in which her team deliberately puts effort into developing and maintaining its unity and care. She tells how they meet regularly for prayer and fellowship. In a recent meeting God spoke to them of the need to be free from bondages of the past. 'At times like these we see ourselves in our most vulnerable state, breaking down without any inhibitions, stripped of all our defences. We've clearly seen God bringing us closer to one another as we've leaned and cried on each other's shoulders.' On another occasion she shared how the team met in preparation for going on a prayer walk. 'As we waited on the Lord to guide us He led us into an extended time of prayer for one another. We postponed the prayer walk till later, giving priority to our team fellowship.'

Teams and individuals within the family of WEC recognise our God-given oneness. We value it, promote it, guard it and deliberately make every effort to maintain it. We confess we haven't always succeeded, but if we lose it it's always there to be claimed afresh at the foot of the cross.

How a crisis was handled

A WEC field in West Africa was in crisis. A deep division had developed over the issue of missionaries adopting national children. Two workers had done this, but the adopted girls' lives were a bad testimony and the other missionaries were clamouring for action because this reflected badly on the mission's reputation.

Norman Grubb asked a WECer from another West African field to visit these workers. He agreed to do so and wrote in his report:

Half the fellowship said, 'Deal with that, we're up against it. It's a bad testimony.' The other half said, 'If you throw them out then we'll resign.'

We knew the answer was to go to prayer. We arrived there on the Monday and went to prayer Monday night. We were supposed to have business discussions but we never got down to these. All day Tuesday it was nothing but prayer and waiting on God. On the Wednesday there was still no business session. This thing was so monstrous that we kept praying all day Wednesday. About 10 pm I dismissed the group. Some went home, others stayed to pray and my wife and I stayed with them.

We urged, 'You've all got your treasures, your convictions. Are you not willing to put them on the altar? Don't worry about a thing. If they're not good the Lord will throw them away, but if they are all right He'll keep them.'

So, one by one they started coming forward putting their convictions on the altar. 'I've been strong-headed on this but now I'm giving it to the Lord.'

As it started to break, someone went and woke the others. 'Hey, come back, the Lord's breaking through.' And He broke through that night – it was a tremendous experience. The Lord spoke to the missionaries who had adopted the girls and told them they had to ask for leave of absence in order to get their house in order. They weren't being thrown out so nobody had anything to grumble about! God broke through in a marvellous way.

This story is another proof that the way of openness and brokenness coupled with earnest prayer for God's will to be revealed, is the key to maintaining and deepening fellowship.

9

The Real Work is Prayer

Stewart Dinnen

Core Value: *We are convinced that prayer is a priority*

When Norman Grubb came home from Congo to take over as leader of WEC's only sending base, he had a concern about the pattern of life at the London headquarters. Workers would meet in the morning to read a passage of scripture and then spend a few minutes committing the activities of the field and base to the Lord in prayer. Then it was off to work in the office and various departments.

This set him thinking. Wasn't the real work getting through to God in faith for growth and blessing, and in taking a stand against entrenched forces of evil on the field? So he instituted some radical changes.

Strategic praying

The fellowship started to meet at 9am, firstly for a 'dig' into the Word, then a sharing of mission news including a frank statement about specific problems and pressures. After that came a free discussion, with questions and comments (even from the newest candidates) leading to a consensus about what the Lord's leading might be regarding the issues raised. Then – and only then – did they go to their knees to press through in faith to a point where there was praise and expectancy that God's power would be released to accomplish what they had sensed to be His will.

In those early years – in the thirties, forties and fifties – the mission grew by leaps and bounds. Getting through to God in prayer enabled the team to rise in faith for advances into new fields, the calling of recruits, and the supply of resources to make the new steps possible.

Does faith really release the power of God? Look at these biblical instances:

- The friends of the paralysed man had faith to believe that Jesus would heal him (Luke 5:18-25).
- The centurion had faith to say to Jesus that He did not need to come to his house to heal his servant (Luke 7:6-10).
- The bent-over woman had faith for healing as she touched Jesus' coat (Luke 8:43-48).
- The blind man had faith that Jesus could heal him (Luke 18:39-43).

In each of these cases, Jesus took note and remarked about their faith. But after calming the waves in the storm on the lake, the Lord rebuked the disciples for their lack of faith (Luke 8:22-25).

Does the same system continue in WEC today? Well, with the development of other bases and fields, and the great distances separating workers, the exact pattern instituted at the London headquarters is impossible to follow, but wherever workers gather – for conferences, retreats, or for informal times of fellowship – prayer is an increasingly dominant feature. With the arrival of many Brazilians and Koreans into the mission, their emphasis on prayer has blessed and reinvigorated WEC's prayer life.

But it is not prayer for prayer's sake: it is prayer that

a) is an expression of worship,
b) leads to faith,
c) exercises authority in standing against the works of the enemy.

A few years ago the leaders of our European sending bases were at the crossroads. They all sensed a burden for the commencement of a WEC training college but personnel and property were major hurdles. So they trusted the Lord for an initial confirmation in the form of a suitably qualified WECer coming forward to head up the project. This happened within a year. They met again: property was needed but where should it be? Before the deadline they had set, sufficient gifts came in for the purchase of a suitable property that had become available in the Netherlands.

Warfare praying

There is, however, a far wider and more intense aspect to prayer, and that is spiritual warfare. In 2 Corinthians 10:4 Paul says, 'The weapons we fight with are not the weapons of the world. On the contrary, they have divine power to demolish strongholds.' The very nature of mission is conflict – the power of God's kingdom versus the powers of darkness. The last thing Satan wants to do is to release territory to the Lord. So our workers need to know how to *recognise* his activities, *resist* him (as Jesus teaches in Matthew 12:29), and *rely* on the finished work of Calvary, at which satanic forces were routed (Revelation 12:11).

In Burkina Faso, mission work was thwarted for years because the tribal initiation rites carried out on the young men resulted in their becoming impervious to the gospel. Workers sent out a call to our sending bases for warfare prayer, binding the forces of evil before the next ceremonies came round. By that time, two of the chiefs involved had died, two others had become Christians, and the government had stepped in with a decree that the ceremonies could last only a few days instead of a month as previously.

Bruce Rattray from Australia, and Jambi, an ex-animist Dayak and son of a witch doctor, worked well together in the occult-ridden culture of Kalimantan. Jambi had learned how to use his authority against demons, and things went well for a time. But he backslid and Bruce lost contact with him until one day they met in the village of Merakai.

'I want to talk to you,' Jambi said. Bruce felt that this was unusually direct for a Dayak.

'It's very easy to slip away from the Lord, but it's very hard to come back again,' Jambi continued. 'I have a problem. My dad, who was a very well-known witch doctor in this area, died a few months ago, and every time I sit down to eat he appears at the table. How am I supposed to handle this?'

Bruce replied: 'Don't you remember what I taught you? When a person dies in Christ he goes to Paradise; if a person dies out of Christ he goes to Hades. So it can't be your dad.'

'Well, I ought to be able to recognise my own father,' said Jambi.

Bruce responded: 'It is not your father. It is an evil spirit impersonating him. The spirit knew your father very well because he was a witch-doctor.'

'What shall I do?' asked Jambi.

Bruce made a proposal. 'We will pray together. I will lead you in prayer deliberately commanding this spirit to leave and never return. Do you understand that?'

'Yes, I understand. I remember you taught me that before.'

Bruce prayed: 'Dear Father, in the name of the Lord Jesus Christ we bind the power of Satan and specifically command the evil spirit impersonating Jambi's father to go where Jesus Christ would send it and never come back again. We claim total deliverance for Jambi as a blood-bought child of God, and take the victory that has already been won by Jesus on Calvary.'

Ten days later Bruce met up with Jambi again and asked him, 'How is that problem with your dad appearing at meals?'

Jambi replied, 'That's gone. He's not returned again.'

Three levels of prayer are discernible in Acts. Chapter 13 describes what could be called strategic prayer, as the leaders of the Antioch church waited on God; this led to Paul and Barnabas being sent out. Chapter 12 describes an intercessory prayer meeting when the church in Jerusalem took faith for the release of Peter from prison. Chapter 4 contains warfare prayer as the church recognises evil forces arrayed against it, so takes faith for gospel advance (4: 23-31).

But it is not just a matter of WEC workers praying. We have been greatly blessed by an army of praying people who have gone out of their way to give time and energy to get to know the situations in which WECers work, to understand the spiritual issues and believe God for the breakthrough.

Prayer is central; prayer is crucial; prayer is the key to faith, to advance, and to victory over the enemy. As long as we keep it that way, WEC will continue to be used by the Lord for the extension of His kingdom.

Do you believe a wooden face has the power to kill?

Graham Chalker

We were driving into a village when, all of a sudden, people started yelling out to Janet to close her eyes. At the same time we looked toward the village where we saw something that we – or at least Janet – shouldn't have seen.

At the heart of the animistic religion is the worship of idols and fetishes. If this worship is carried out according to the whims of these capricious gods, peace and prosperity will be the reward. The slightest infraction necessitates an elaborate (and very expensive) ritual to appease the offended god. These gods are represented physically by wooden carvings or human-like figures or, more prevalent in our area, hideous wooden masks. If the villagers want to curry favour with their god, they will take the mask and place it on a designated dancer, who is completely covered in an outfit of straw. As he dances through the village (with what I have no hesitation in describing as supernatural strength), the villagers will sing and dance in adoration of their god. This is a man's show – it is absolutely forbidden for any woman ever to see this mask. They all have to stay indoors. If, accidentally, a woman does happen to see it, she will die – and this does happen!

Janet had seen the mask and everyone in the village knew it. One village elder approached us, and said to Janet in a solemn, but dispassionate way, 'You will die'. Nothing could strip you of all the bravado associated with being a super-spiritual-missionary-in-the-service-of-God quite like those words. This was no idle, glib superstition. His statement was based on a reality that these people live out daily. It quite unnerved both of us.

Do you believe a wooden face has the power to kill? We do, because we believe that behind these things is the power of the one who by nature is a destroyer and murderer – Satan. By prayer we took refuge in the One who disarmed all the principalities and powers (Colossians 2:13-15 RSV).

Three weeks later, we had an unexpected visit from one of the Christian elders from this village. When he saw Janet, he shrieked. He couldn't contain his joy that Janet was still alive. Straightaway we started planning an evangelistic campaign targeting this village and two neighbouring ones, using a film called The Combat (and Janet) as our focal point.

The Christian ladies in these three villages were so excited when we arrived in their villages and saw Janet with me. It was very moving. Following three days of evangelism, the sixty or so Christians who make up these three little churches, had another eighty people wanting to know more about this POWER that conquered their mask.

'There's no one like you'

Louis and Susan Sutton

Dr. Louis and Susan Sutton, Christian servants in Chad, relate the details of a journey in which God worked miracles for them and their three children.

Our seven-year-old, Susan, became very ill four days before Christmas. She showed signs of pressure in her brain and we knew she needed immediate medical attention. What followed was the longest four days of our lives. We prayed and claimed the verse in 2 Chronicles 14:11, 'Lord, there is no one like you to help the powerless against the mighty.'

Could we convince the French military to fly us out? They agreed since the earlier regular flight had been delayed!

'Lord, there is no one like you!'

We flew to the capital. Susan was losing the sight in her left eye and was very weak … only two flights out per week. During Christmas week, of all times, how can a family of five find space on a flight? At the last minute, the airline decided to use a larger plane.

'Lord, there is no one like you!'

We left Chad for France. Susan was blind in the left eye. Louis put her on steroids and we prayed with God's peace. Waiting for the one o'clock flight, Louis checked at the desk. The airline was on strike – NO flights out! We remembered God's faithfulness and prayed. In half an hour the strike was called off!

'Lord, there is no one like you!

Four days after leaving Adre we touched down in Charlotte, North Carolina.

Susan's condition proved to be baffling [but] within days began to show improvement, and within five weeks, her eyesight in the left eye was 20/40 and she had recovered all her seven-year-old energy.

10

Firm at the Centre, Fluid at the Edges

Dore Schupak

Core Value: *We uphold biblical truth and standards.*

One of the biggest problems in the Church today is the way we judge other Christians on some point of theology or their worship style. Imagine working in an organisation of about 2,000 members! How do we cope?

Here we stand

We have agreed to work with each other as Christian brothers and sisters and as equals, even though we may not agree on every single detail of doctrine and practice within Christianity. Some matters of doctrine, however, are non-negotiable. If they are lost, our whole faith is gone. Many have given up the historic pillars of Christian faith in favour of some popular or convenient new teaching. We are committed to avoiding that in WEC! So we have staked out our common beliefs, those upon which all WECers agree, and which we teach in all our churches and Bible schools.

Here are some of our basics. (A fuller statement appears in our *Principles and Practice*.)

- There is one God, and He is the Creator of all things (Genesis 1:1; Exodus 20:11).

- God is manifested in three Persons: the Father, the Son, and the Holy Spirit (Genesis 1:26; John 1:1; 2 Corinthians 13:14).

- The Bible, from Genesis to Revelation, is the inspired Word of God, the supreme authority, fully trustworthy and without error in the original manuscripts (Isaiah 40:8; 2 Timothy 3:16).

- Humanity fell when Adam and Eve, who had been created by God (Psalm 100:3; Mark 10:6), gave in to the temptation in the garden (Genesis 3:17).

- Christ came into the world, born of a virgin (Matthew 1:23), lived a sinless life (1 Peter 2:22), and died for sinners (1 Corinthians 15:3; 1 Timothy 1:15, 2:6). He was crucified, buried and on the third day rose from the dead (Matthew 27:35; 28:6; 1 Corinthians 15:20).

- We are saved through faith in Him (Galatians 2:16) because He alone is the way to God (Acts 4:12), and all who believe will never perish (John 10:28).

- The Holy Spirit can enable ordinary Christians to please and serve God (John 16:13-14).
- While believers enjoy eternal life in heaven, in the presence of the Lord (Psalm 16:11; John 6:47), unbelievers suffer eternal torment away from God's presence (Matthew 25:46; Revelation 20:15).
- The Lord Jesus is coming back again to receive His saints unto Himself (Acts 1:11; 1 Thessalonians 4:16-17).
- We have a responsibility to preach the gospel to all peoples (Matthew 28:19-20; Acts 1:8).
- God is able to meet our every need when we are serving Him in obedience (Psalm 37:25; Philippians 4:19).

The main emphasis

It is important that we keep the saving of souls and establishing Christ's kingdom as our main emphasis! The Bible teaches that, 'If anyone has material possessions and sees his brother in need but has no pity on him, how can the love of God be in him?' (1 John 3:17). While WEC is involved in holistic ministry, demonstrating the compassion of Christ in practical ways to a needy world, we will not be swept up by the latest social or political cause or trend, no matter how important or right it may seem! The scriptures say, 'The world and its desires pass away, but the man who does the will of God lives forever' (1 John 2:17).

Ideas regarding modes of worship or baptism, ecclesiology, spiritual gifts, eschatology, etc., vary from one WECer to another. But these differences are so small in comparison with what we hold in common as to be hardly noticeable.

There have been times when we have had to clarify our position on spiritual gifts, Calvinism/Arminianism, creation/evolution, church order and methods. There may be tensions, but we have felt the important thing is to stand steadily on the middle ground of our beliefs and objectives and through God's grace we have experienced a wonderful sense of unity and fellowship. It is common for WECers not even to know what their teammates' convictions are on secondary matters as we are all busy about the work of glorifying God through serving Him.

Freedom to be fluid

Having committed ourselves to remaining firm at the centre, we then give ourselves leeway to be 'fluid at the edges' in methods and strategies. We are an international, inter-ethnic and inter-denominational fellowship. We have people from over fifty countries working in more than seventy countries around the globe. WECers range in age from late teens (short-termers) to near the century mark (retirees).

The challenge for WEC has been this: how do we maintain our identity and core values and yet stay supple so that we can respond to the myriad of opportunities in today's world? How do we retain the flexibility to react in the way the Holy Spirit guides and not in the way mission protocol dictates? We believe the secret is to stay 'firm at the centre' and 'fluid at the edges'.

As far as the statements of faith above are concerned, our feet are set in concrete. We have no room for compromise. But as far as the **how** of mission is concerned – how we will carry out our commission – we are fluid and adaptable.

The core values outlined in this book define WEC and make it the organisation that it is. Our *Principles and Practice* is thinner than the volume you now hold in your hands. We have aimed to keep our rules to a minimum in order to maximise the liberty given to fields and to individual workers.

A rigid, inflexible business, ministry or church is bound to be left behind in these fast-changing times. Real and felt needs of both workers and those to whom we minister are constantly changing. We want to do our utmost to reach out to people in the many cultures in which we work in ways to which they can relate, with ministries that meet present needs. Front-line WEC activities include not only traditional ministries such as preaching, literature distribution and Bible translation, but also medical work, service to HIV and AIDS sufferers, rehabilitation of alcoholics and drug addicts, and ministry to children on the streets of the world's mega-cities. The practical aspect of our fieldwork is guided by this goal: *Churches planted on every field and every worker a soul-winner.* This is the principle we keep in mind when considering the validity of new ministries. It has kept us on track for nearly 100 years, and will continue to do so as long as God enables us to persevere!

The inner secret

How do we stay together and keep away from strife and dissension, maintaining unity and focus in our work? Not by 'top-down' directives but rather, in humility, putting the Bible and its standards first. So then it is all about obeying Christ's command to love one another! 'Do not think of yourself more highly than you ought, but rather think of yourself with sober judgment, in accordance with the measure of faith God has given you' (Romans 12:3). 'You, then, why do you judge your brother? Or why do you look down on your brother? For we will all stand before God's judgment seat' (Romans 14:10). 'Each of you should look not only to your own interests, but also to the interests of others' (Philippians 2:4).

Here are instances in which fluidity has paid off:

- In recent years a growing concern has arisen in many sending base churches for a greater participation in their missionaries' careers, even though they are working with interdenominational agencies. This has led to them asking for a greater say in the workers' placement and ministry.

   So we have had a change of policy in WEC resulting in a more consultative approach with home churches. For instance, church leaders are now invited to attend and observe the all-important process of considering candidates from their churches for acceptance after the orientation course.

- Over many years WEC has been in the business of planting and nurturing churches along traditional lines, with public worship services as a central feature. More recently, a team in a country whose government is hostile to Christianity has embraced a different pattern in which the key unit is the cell group. These are informal groups meeting in homes, and are trained to be ready to split once they reach a certain size in order to preserve a low profile.

The Bible and a common biblical basis of belief is our anchor. All must agree to this foundation. Beyond that we realise it is by prayer, listening to each other, studying biblical principles, living godly lives and understanding local needs that we can be led as a united fellowship into effective service.

Finding the way through

Stewart Dinnen

There have been some big challenges to our doctrinal unity.

In the seventies, the Holy Spirit was at work through the growth of **the charismatic movement.** But weren't people in WEC from a range of conservative evangelical churches and some from Pentecostal churches? Had the gifts of the Spirit ceased with the last of the Apostles? To be filled with the Spirit did all have to speak in tongues? You can imagine the discussions! What were we to do? Many churches and Christian organisations split over the issues.

Robert Mackey, WEC's International Director, opened the subject up by sending a questionnaire to all WEC fields and sending bases encouraging genuine openness. At the 1978 International Conference in Scotland, the results of the survey were shared and, in a spirit of frankness and open discussion coupled with much prayer, the issues were faced. In a remarkable way, guiding principles were laid down and unity was preserved. (*International Guidelines: Team Manual I,* WEC International).

Of course we have not been without our strong protagonists in various camps but only a very few resigned, the vast majority accepting the mission's final statement on the issue, leading to fruitfulness and effectiveness in ministry.

In the eighties and the nineties, the vexed question of **divorce** surfaced as we were faced with applications from those who were in this category. Should we accept a person who had been separated, or one who had been divorced and remarried, or one who had been divorced twice and remarried? Should a person who had been divorced while a Christian and remarried be received into WEC? What would our WEC-founded churches feel?

As can be imagined there was a strong emotional element as people knew individuals personally and were concerned about consequences for them and the testimony of Christ.

Again thorough research was done and information obtained from other organisations which had gone through a similar struggle. At the International Conferences in 1984 and 1996, Stewart Dinnen and Dieter Kuhl, successive International Directors, encouraged a climate of genuine desire to find what scripture did and didn't say.

After a prolonged period of prayer, interaction and, most of all, a thorough study of the Bible, we came to a conclusion that we feel has given a clear mandate in love and truth.

Body Beautiful

Mady Vaillant

Core Value: *We affirm our love for Christ's church and endeavour to work in fellowship with local and national churches, and with other Christian agencies.*

C.T. Studd, the founder of WEC, had a strong conviction that WEC had been raised up by God to do a job in places where there were gaps in fulfilling the Great Commission. This led to his idea that WEC could be called 'Christ's Etceteras' and he wrote a booklet explaining his theory (*Christ's Etceteras*, WEC International). He felt that everyone who joined WEC must be convinced that they should 'love all who love the Lord sincerely without partiality, and to love all people.' This has led to a respect for the church worldwide and a desire to co-operate with other Christian agencies.

Where the rubber often hits the road is when fruit in evangelism and discipleship results in a growing church. What should be the relationship between it and the church planter?

Crisis time

Kneeling in her bedroom, the field leader felt overwhelmed with grief. She had spent a quarter of a century working in West Africa and she, along with other colleagues, had given her best under very trying circumstances. The Lord had blessed; the church of Christ was born, had grown for a while, and now everything seemed to be going wrong. The tension between missionaries and church was unbearable. Misunderstandings, accusations and hurt feelings were piling up. They had tried several times to put things right but to no avail.

It seemed to her that she and her team were navigating in uncharted waters. Hidden rocks were everywhere and she could find no landmarks left by her predecessors. Already several times the fellowship had been damaged by these reefs.

She wept before the Lord and prayed: 'There must be a way through all this, a well-marked channel that will enable us to come out of these turbulent waters in one piece and in a way glorifying to the Lord. Show us, Lord!'

There was no doubt in her mind that WEC was founded and, to this day, is thriving on the four pillars of sacrifice, faith, holiness and fellowship. She sensed that it was within these parameters that the solution was to be found, for these principles were just as valid for relationships with the WEC-related church as between WECers.

'Loving Christ's church and endeavouring to work in fellowship with local and national churches' is easy to say and logical, especially for people appointed to be co-workers with Christ in bringing His church to birth. Why is it then so difficult?

There are probably several reasons:

Political changes

In West African history the scene changed from slavery to colonialism, then, in the 1960s, from colonialism to independence. Slavery and colonialism both left scars. Even if a Christian agency is not directly responsible for the hurts caused there are often underlying accusations against those from the former colonising nations. We must not forget that school textbooks nowadays relate with great detail the hardship and cruelty Africans endured in the past, so the memory of it is kept alive. We should not be surprised, then, if young Christians have to work their way through all these negative feelings towards the foreigner.

Independence was seen as the beginning of a new era in which Africans would, at long last, be able to handle their own destiny. Today, although some countries show definite economic and social progress, many others struggle with civil wars, huge burdens of debt, millions of refugees, poverty, famine, and AIDS.

How does the church fare in all this?

The desire to be independent of the mission is there and rightly so, for dependency is a sign of immaturity. But the all-important word here is balance. It is too easy for the pendulum to swing to another extreme. Is not interdependency God's best in church/mission relationships? I believe it is, and that calls for a balanced attitude on both parts. That can only be acquired as we work at it – and it is a hard task for all concerned!

Relationship changes

As the pioneering era passed, a parent-child relationship emerged with the church needing to be carefully nurtured.

What the church wants in most countries is a partnership relationship with the mission. This is a participatory relationship in which the mission is simply a part of the church and works in a complementary manner with it. Isn't this what mission is all about? To bring the Good News to those who have never heard it, to see the church come into being, to nurture it and see it come to maturity and start reaching out to the unreached? Some believe the missionary should move on to starting the same pattern elsewhere. But the truth is that often much strengthening still needs to be done in training and strategising. In poverty-stricken countries a sharing of material assets from the privileged countries of the world may still be needed, but that needs to be done wisely, in consultation with the church, and without encouraging financial dependence.

Attitude changes

In any good relationship strenuous efforts to understand each other are necessary. Church/mission relationships are no exception. Either party can so easily fall into criticism of the other, and that is deadly. The Word of God calls us to have genuine respect and esteem for each other at all times. Another area in which both mission and church need to cooperate is in making available to each other the means and abilities to achieve their corporate goals.

On the mission's side, to love Christ's church and work in fellowship with it means greater humility and flexibility in continually accepting the host culture as being different but not inferior. Mistakes have been made in the past. Can we honestly recognise them, even if they were made by our predecessors, and seek forgiveness? The Lord has given different gifts to us all. We need to recognise that our WEC-related church people are often better equipped for the work than we expatriates, for they function in their home environment. As a result, they often do the job better than we can, even if they use different methods.

To love the church we also need to live in transparency with it and learn to trust those we may have brought to Christ. That also means making decisions together in all kinds of areas such as recruitment, orientation of new workers, placement, dismissal, goal setting and projects.

It would be wrong to think that changes of attitude are only needed in the mission. The church, too, needs to break free from a feeling of oppression and inability to cope. To believe in and use the potential the Lord has given them will enable national Christians to give the lie to the commonly held belief that the church is too poor to function without outside help.

The church needs to be aware of the strong retro-colonialism syndrome that 'all ills come from the Whites', and refuse to let it influence its relationship with expatriate missionaries.

It took a while for the WEC leader to discover these truths and start practising them. One of the first landmarks she was given was to 'live a life worthy of the calling you have received. Be completely humble and gentle; be patient, bearing with one another in love. Make every effort to keep the unity of the Spirit through the bond of peace' (Ephesians 4:1-4). That was the way she needed to go. It was costly but proved to be the right way. Relationships improved to such an extent that today love continues to flow through church to mission and vice versa.

Progress!

In some places the church has grown in steady strides as in Congo, Colombia, Ivory Coast and parts of Asia. In other places it has been slow and discouraging as in Japan, the Middle East and Southern Europe. The challenge has been to help the newly developing churches through the pioneering, parenting, partnership and participatory stages. Sometimes there are problems for cross-cultural workers who don't want to work themselves out of a job or hand over all aspects of church life as soon as practicable. The temptation is to say that the Christians or the church are not mature enough – but by whose standard can that be measured?

In the sending countries

At sending centres worldwide, where new workers are recruited and prayer and other kinds of support are needed, the Christian sending agency has to work hand in hand with local, evangelical churches. They are on the same side and, although given different areas of focus, there must be trust and cooperation, not competition. WEC has tried to love all those who love the Lord sincerely without partiality, and to work with local churches through consultation and cooperation. Joint missionary conventions, prayer times, teaching ministries, acceptance of candidates and consultations about the pastoral care of the workers have all been part of this process. WEC aims to give to and bless the church.

With other agencies

One of the great privileges of cross-cultural ministry has been the possibility of working with other like-minded organisations. Respect, communication and seeing the big picture are crucial to make this work.

Stewart Dinnen, former principal of WEC's Missionary Training College in Australia and International Director, gives the following examples of co-operation between agencies:

- WEC often seconds (loans) workers to other missions that may be in need of the help those individuals can give. Typical of this would be the secondment of an Australian WECer to FEBC in Thailand, where she is in charge of radio programming.

- WEC Missionary Training Colleges train their students to serve with many organisations around the world.

- The team in Mexico is fully involved in the promotion and development of Promise Keepers (known locally as Men of Integrity).

- C&MA sponsored WEC into Indonesian Kalimantan and SUM sponsored WEC into Chad.

- In a Middle Eastern country various agencies co-operate so closely that joint teams of workers pioneer new areas.

- A pastor and wife team of the WEC-related church in Congo work as members of the WEC field in Côte d'Ivoire and another couple are part of the Chad field.

- Radio Worldwide, a department of WEC in UK, gives training and professional support to any who wish to become involved in Christian radio.
- Two Italian churches helped in the establishment of a Betel drug rehabilitation centre in Naples.

We are one in the task, co-operation is essential, and trust must be fostered at all costs.

Full circle

Jenny Davies

In 1980 a young man from the country of Guinea went to The Gambia to make some money. He opened a little tailoring shop opposite the home of Anne Kelland and Shirley Strong. He made them some dresses and, along with the payment, they gave him portions of the New Testament. Lamin was fascinated and compared them with the Koran. 'Which came first?' he asked his Koranic teacher. 'The Bible was written first,' the teacher told him. After months of study and thought, Lamin was convinced that Jesus was the only way and received Him as his Lord and Saviour.

Huge changes took place in his life after that decision:

- His young wife and child left him.
- His father came and attacked him.
- He became very sick with TB and was healed.
- On his return to Guinea to explain to his family, he suddenly became very sick (suspected poisoning) and almost died. A last minute call to Jesus and a deep sleep revived him.

Through all these experiences and many others, Lamin steadfastly trusted the Lord and saw answers to prayer. His wife became a Christian and returned to him and so did his mother.

As he grew in spiritual stature he became deeply burdened for his hometown where there was no Christian witness whatsoever. After several years of quiet witnessing and explaining the gospel, he saw a small group believe and form a church.

The Imams were furious and tried to get rid of him and break up the group. One memorable week a decision had been made to kill him on a certain day but God intervened. The night before the deed was to take place, the main instigator suddenly died. This put everyone into fear and confusion and Lamin was spared.

After many trials and opposition Lamin's credibility was gradually seen and accepted by the people. Now there is an active church and leaders and teachers are reaching out to others. A school and youth work have been established. The gospel is spreading slowly to the Fula villages in Guinea and beyond.

Lamin is now a consultant to the WEC team and an active participant in the ministry, and many people, both Africans and expatriates, go to him for help and advice.

Men of Integrity

Mike Burnam

The vision for Men of Integrity came out of a deep personal need. When the opportunity came for me to attend a Promise Keepers conference in the United States, I was ready for some radical changes in my life. At that conference I had a close encounter with God and realized that the truths and principles of God's Word which were being presented were universal truths for all men. They concerned:

- A man and his relationship to God
- A man and his relationship to other men for accountability
- A man and his family
- A man and his church
- A man and his brothers
- A man and his world

On my return to Mexico, I gave some Promise Keepers books in Spanish to several of the pastors in our city of Cuernavaca. As they began to read and gain an understanding of the need for men's ministry in the local church, the doors of opportunity began to open. Pastors from different denominations began to see that many of the felt needs in their churches could be met through such a ministry. I began to meet with some of the interested pastors and men and, as we began to explore ways to begin a men's movement in the city, more key pastors were drawn to us.

From the very beginning we thought beyond a city-wide movement to a state-wide and country-wide movement. No one group had all the resources needed to initiate the movement, but together, as a body of Christ, we did. In our first meeting with pastors we presented the vision, but structured it so that others could join in and contribute to the ministry.

We began with a team of seven pastors and missionaries. As we began to teach 'body of Christ' principles to others, we realised that we would be hypocrites if we didn't live them out in our own lives. Some of the pastors sought fellowship with other churches. As a result, churches of several different denominations began to hold joint men's meetings and conferences and we began to produce training materials for pastors and leaders of men's groups.

Our common purpose knitted our souls together and a deep bond of love for one another and for God developed. Although the initial vision had been to impact the church in Mexico through this ministry, other areas of opportunity were opening up as we had gained the credibility to minister on a much broader spectrum of topics. We began to invite others onto the team to use their special gifts in this

Continued

wider ministry. Now teaching and training on missions, discipleship, marriage and evangelism are part of the vision.

As churches began to hear about our unity and teamwork and the seminars and events we were offering, the ministry spread to other cities in the country and even to some outside Mexico. I have no greater joy than to go to a city where the church is fragmented and to see it become a model of the body of Christ. It is such a blessing to hear pastors and leaders say, 'You guys work as a team. We can see that you truly love each other, and the thing that impresses us is that you are all from different denominations. Why is it that in our city even those of us from the same denomination can't get along together?'

As WEC we have some excellent core values that can serve as models for the church of Christ; the harvest is much larger than any mission agency or church can handle. All I can say is that I'm in love with the body of Christ, and nothing gives me more satisfaction than seeing all my brothers – Presbyterian, Methodist, Charismatic, Pentecostal, Baptist and others – loving each other and enjoying the unity that only Christ can give.

12

Flexibility, Frankness and Freedom

Tineke Davelaar and Janny Riemersma

Core Value: *We accept each other irrespective of gender, ethnic background or church affiliation.*

Tineke and Janny became two of WEC's many wise and fruitful women leaders. They relate some of their experiences and observations of working with men and women from other countries and church backgrounds.

If there was anything that particularly drew us to WEC, it was the recognition that there was a place for everyone in missionary service. Reading biographies of WECers and looking at the lives of WEC people we knew, we were convinced that flexibility was an important characteristic of the mission.

Does the practice of working together with others called to the same mission, irrespective of their gender, ethnic or church background, create difficulties? What if the other person doesn't understand our way of thinking? What if someone isn't sure he can listen to a woman preach? What if another doesn't agree with something I say?

The exhortation of the apostle Paul to the Ephesian Church is relevant to the missionary community: 'Make every effort to keep the unity of the Spirit through the bond of peace ... There is one Lord, one faith, one baptism, one God and Father of all, who is over all and through all and in all' (Ephesians 4:3-6). In his book, *Love Covers,* Paul Billheimer says that fellowship between born-again believers should be on the basis of a common origin, a common parenthood, and a common family relationship rather than on a common opinion in non-essentials.

We have certainly been enriched by the variety of cultural values, national characteristics, church traditions and practices exhibited by our colleagues. But yes, it's true, there are different ways of thinking and it's possible to unknowingly offend or be misunderstood. Living and working together on the field is a learning experience of living out Romans 15:7: 'Accept one another, then, just as Christ has accepted you.'

Acceptance is not dependent on gender

In WEC it is recognised that there is as much room for women as for men to develop their gifts since 'In Christ there is neither male nor female' (Galatians 3:28). There are fields where women are in leadership, and we happen to have been the leaders in one of them. None of the men had any objections, and we were strongly supported by our international leaders. History also shows that in WEC both married and single women have been pioneers and have been recognised in the ministry role God had given them.

Women are allowed to plant churches. In practice it seems that churches planted by women come more quickly under indigenous leadership as women are keen to hand over their responsibilities to local men. Often women do not consider preaching unless they are put on the spot. As Janny experienced:

I went to Kalimantan wanting to use medical work as a means of evangelism. I thought that was all I could do. When colleagues moved away, a national evangelist and I led the church, so I started preaching every other Sunday. It was then that I found out that I loved passing on Christian doctrines and principles from the Bible. Later I taught in a Bible school. We feel very much blessed to be in a mission where a woman can fulfil the ministry God has given her.

Acceptance is not dependent on ethnic background

Something of the manifold wisdom of God (Ephesians 3:10) is shown when people from many nations and church backgrounds can work together.

Workers expect to have to adjust to the culture of the new country but are surprised when they find out that adjusting to the culture and thought patterns of colleagues is included in the package. We are mentally prepared to adjust to the local culture but we may be part of an international team. Things may be done quite differently by our co-workers and their values are often different from ours.

Janny explains:

I prepared myself for work in Indonesia by attending a Bible college in Britain to learn how people lived in another country. But I still came across different customs and values in the missionary team. Birthdays didn't seem to be as important to some people as they are in Holland. And when I had proudly made my first batch of biscuits (cookies for the Americans!) my eyes nearly popped out when a colleague apparently liked them so much that he ate one after the other. In Holland you offer a biscuit with each cup of coffee and close the lid of the tin in between. Having a sense of humour and a good dose of flexibility is essential.

Because the thought patterns of Asians and Westerners differ so much, it is possible to offend without being aware of it. I remember asking an Indonesian church elder whether he had passed on some money to the Bible school when he came back from a trip. (A staff member of the school had told me that she had not received it.) I thought that perhaps he had given the money to another person. Unknown to me, the elder was furious and wrote several letters to the head of the Synod and the Bible school. In his mind I had accused him of stealing. When I finally heard about it, I went to him immediately and apologised profusely. His anger abated and we were able to discuss the western and eastern mindset.

Many Asians are serving in WEC today and differences of western and eastern patterns of thinking and expectations may at times cause offence. For healthy relationships it is imperative to follow Matthew 5:23-24: 'If you remember that your brother has something against you, leave your gift there in front of the altar. First go and be reconciled with your brother.'

Tineke adds:

Even Christmas can cause problems! Celebrations can be held in many different ways, with lots of presents, food and laughter, or with a sober meal and no presents.

Then we can easily carry prejudice against a particular nationality. One dear colleague had had difficult experiences with people from my country in the past. She thought we must all be alike and had allowed prejudice to spring up in her heart and this affected her relationship with me. It came to a climax, and she shared how she felt in her heart towards me. We still had to work through some issues, but from that time on our relationship improved.

There are many positives about working with colleagues from many countries. We've learnt hospitality from the Asians and how to take time for food and fellowship. We've learnt to invite people for a meal instead of just a Dutch cup of coffee. Hospitality is an important trait in many countries and we're learning that from our colleagues as well as from our host culture. The Americans have taught us to use encouraging words. 'You did a good job there' makes us feel needed and important and spurs us on in the work. How far an encouraging word goes! It does not come easily to the Dutch, but we are learning.

Acceptance is not dependent on church affiliation

In our experience we have found that we've been able to work with WECers from many different church backgrounds. Often we haven't even known the denomination of a colleague. It didn't seem to matter. We worked together in harmony.

Janny says:

It has been truly amazing that we've been able to plant churches without too many difficulties related to Bible doctrines and church practices. Although from different church backgrounds, from charismatic to non-charismatic, as a team we have been able to serve the church and even teach in its Bible school.

We trust that the students have learnt what are important fundamental doctrines and what are peripheral matters in which Christians can agree to differ.

Tineke recalls:

I had a hard time accepting the traditional kind of church service on our field. After all, I had left that kind of traditionalism behind me. Going to church became a chore until one of the missionaries said to me, 'I can tell by your face that you are not enjoying the services.' That hit me hard and brought me to my knees. After all, the Lord knew all about the church situation. I had to work through my critical spirit regarding this issue and the Lord really helped me to feel more and more part of the fellowship and to accept my co-workers and local brothers and sisters in the Lord.

Yes, we have proved that we can accept each other irrespective of gender, ethnic background or church affiliation.

Gender on the agenda

Truus Wierda

The issue of gender discrimination has enormous significance in most Islamic countries. In this postscript, a lady doctor who, with her surgeon husband, has worked in a Middle East country for many years, pulls the curtain back on efforts to improve the situation of women who have deep physical and spiritual needs.

Muslim women are not in a position to make independent decisions. The father decides whether, and for how long, his daughter goes to school. The parents decide on the marriage partner, and after marriage the husband makes the major decisions. A wise and loving father will try to find a good husband for his daughter, a selfish or foolish man may 'sell' his daughter to a completely unsuitable partner.

Fortunately many kind husbands learn to love and appreciate their wives and take their wishes into consideration. But there are also harsh and demanding men. Some women live with the constant fear of abuse, divorce, or a second wife being brought into the house. Of course there are also many sad family situations in western countries, but there women have at least equal legal status. Here the law favours and protects men. In case of divorce, the husband always receives custody of the children over a certain age.

Continued

If a man falls ill, he drives to the nearest hospital or goes by public transport to a health centre. A sick woman depends on her husband or male relatives to take her to the doctor. Right from the start we have tried to make our health care services easily accessible for women. We see them separately in a women's clinic where, away from the eyes of men, they can unveil and unwind. Many of them are pregnant, and usually all are tired, anaemic and overworked because of many pregnancies and large families. A listening ear and a friendly word make a lot of difference. I can hear you say, 'It must be wonderful to serve these underprivileged ladies.' It certainly is a challenge! But any prospective colleagues should take a course in crowd control and martial arts. Unfortunately the practice of queuing is not very popular. Quite often a mob of veiled figures struggles and pushes its way into the women's clinic, and it takes much patience (often more than we can muster!) plus stamina to handle them in a kind and dignified manner.

If a woman needs complicated surgery, her outlook is even bleaker. It is so much easier for a man to travel to the capital or even abroad, than for a woman. It is so good to have a very skilled surgeon here. He has done some amazing operations on women who otherwise would probably never have had the opportunity to have surgery. One fifty-year-old lady had her cleft lip beautifully repaired. A little girl with a crippled foot (the result of a car accident) is able to walk again. A lady who had undergone three unsuccessful operations for a vesico-vaginal fistula (a condition caused by complicated childbirth, resulting in leakage of urine) was finally cured and able to live a normal life.

To share the Good News with these women is difficult. Even if their male guardians don't object, most of the women have not learned to think for themselves; sometimes you hear them say in the clinic, 'We are only cows!' We believe that the love and compassion shown to them in the name of the Lord can touch their hearts.

13

Multicultural – Many Clashes?

Jonathan Chamberlain

Core Value: *We desire to work in multicultural teams and are committed to effective international co-operation.*

Here are a handful of comments from non-Westerners who have joined WEC:

'Somewhere we had a nagging feeling we were different, and that others were looking at us with a different eye.'

'Even simple things left me confused.'

'You feel stupid.'

'You may be trying to speak English but are still thinking Chinese. And there are big differences with non-verbal cues too.'

'In some Westerners I sense a general feeling of superiority, even though it is unconscious most of the time.'

'When they signalled me to come with a gesture that seems very rude in my culture, I reacted strongly. They in turn were not very patient with me.'

Multicultural teams? No way, José!

God's idea

We never planned to become a multicultural mission. True, after its initial founding in 1913 as a British mission, WEC bases were soon established in other Western and European countries. But we only saw ourselves as a Western organisation until God started to wake us up to the new global reality. In the 1950s Horace Williams, WEC missionary to Taiwan, began to urge the mission to recruit Chinese to evangelise mainland China. Nothing happened. In fact the dominant feeling was that WEC should encourage the birthing of indigenous national missions in non-Western countries where the church was firmly established. Leslie Brierley, International Director for Research, actually moved to Brazil in 1971 for a three-year stint to facilitate such a movement. This he did, but Brazilians still wanted to know how they could join WEC!

From 1961 onwards successive leaders' conferences gradually recognised that WEC would bring into its ranks more non-Westerners. By 1981 the leaders declared, 'The Lord is leading us to become an increasingly multiracial fellowship in order to fulfil our mandate of worldwide evangelisation. We recognise and accept the possibility that we may not be a predominantly Western mission.'

By the mid-seventies a steady flow of non-Westerners were joining us. From 1982 the rate rapidly increased. Sending bases were established in Brazil in 1978, and Singapore in 1982. Others followed: Hong Kong (1986), Taiwan (1990), Indonesia (1994), Korea (1995) and Venezuela (1999). People called by God from a plethora of nations are steadily becoming part of the family. Fijians and Finnish, Malaysians and Mauritians, Canadians and Colombians, Indonesians and Irish, and thirty-nine others! By the year 2002 nearly 350 WECers originated from the non-Western world. One in four WECers are non-Caucasian. It wasn't WEC's idea; it was God's.

Team mix

People serving with WEC find themselves thrown into teams of many cultures. One new team of five members represents five different nationalities! Cambodia has had a team of workers made up of people from Brazil, Singapore, Korea, UK, USA, France and Australia. At one time the team in Senegal was composed of twelve nationalities. Today, forty-eight nations are represented in WEC.

Why bother?

So, is this exotic cultural variety sheer heaven? Not exactly. Working together without falling apart is usually hard work, sometimes traumatic, and occasionally fantastic! Why would God want us to walk this way?

We've discovered many good reasons. Working as a multicultural team provides a microcosm of the universal church. We're going to end up living and serving together in the heavenly kingdom anyway, so why not start practising now? Creative methods of ministry can flow as we plan and strategise together. A monocultural team is more likely to impose its own homegrown way of doing things in the field situation. A multicultural team has a built-in protection against this danger. Members from one cultural background often bring complementary strengths to a team – the evangelistic fervour of the Brazilians, the organising skills of the Germans, the business acumen of the Singaporeans, the tireless stamina of the Hong Kongers and the linguistic skills of the Dutch.

Gospel access may be enhanced. Some nationalities may gain visas for restricted countries where others cannot. The ability of near-culture workers to adapt easily to the target culture can prove a real asset to a team.

Perhaps the strongest argument for multicultural teams is the power of their witness. The more we demonstrate our oneness in life and ministry across our cultural divides, the more convincing our message is to unbelievers.

Perfect team

Are our ethnically diverse teams shining examples that Jesus is Lord? We cannot claim this. In fact the late eighties and nineties was a period of struggle as we grappled with the dynamics of multicultural relationships.

One new Asian worker settling into such a team wrote enthusiastically, 'I know this is where He wants me to be, that I'm in the centre of His will, and in the right place, right time, right people group, and right WEC family.' Two years later the same person had relationship problems with the team leader and the team members. She isolated herself, refused to attend the annual field conference and blamed all her problems on the team. This was not an isolated case. Many non-Westerners have struggled to integrate into WEC. The initial resignation rate of Brazilians was discouraging. But we are learning and growing.

In one sense this process of adjustment was not a new experience. Thirty years earlier there was a steep learning curve for different Western nationalities as they worked through their differences. On one field the Europeans thought the American women unspiritual because they wore make-up, while the Americans thought the Europeans unspiritual because they didn't think drinking alcoholic beverages was sinful!

Four essential keys

Former International Director, Dieter Kuhl, says, 'It is a miracle that the Lord has kept us together and that we have had relatively few crises and emergencies because of unbridgeable rifts.' So how do we manage to work harmoniously as multicultural teams? God has taught us a few down-to-earth lessons.

1. Change Wrong Attitudes
   We all tend to over-rate the ways and values of our own culture, seeing them as right, normal and acceptable. This leads to an unconscious attitude of racial superiority, an ethnocentric blindness. The missionary is often prepared to die to his racial pride when it comes to valuing the target culture, but not so ready to do so in regard to his co-workers.

   John wrote from a newly formed team, 'Coming from various countries and backgrounds, it is human to have diverse convictions of how things should be done. Pray that God would grant us humility and patience so that we can work as a team.'

   There is another subtle deception that can often obscure truth. Our cultural differences can easily be made a scapegoat for not getting on together. We have discovered it is easy to label as a cultural problem a clash which has its root in a personality difference, or a generational difference, or a plainly sinful attitude. We may be particularly vulnerable to this during the early period in a foreign culture while coping with the symptoms of culture shock.

2. Build Good Friendships
   Much prejudice, preconceived ideas, and stereotyping of co-workers from

other cultures can best be broken down by building good friendships. This takes time and effort – not just working together but being together in recreational or relaxing settings.

Some of our team leaders have found that a visit to the home country of team members from a very different culture has helped them understand and appreciate them in a whole new way. They come to understand their background and can establish a more meaningful friendship.

One team was initially comprised of Asians from various countries. Receiving their first four Western members, they wisely spent time clarifying mutual expectations. The Asians perceived that Westerners wanted much more privacy than Asians. Were the new workers willing for Asian members to use their home and to drop in and out without appointments? They covered a lot of issues in a time of open sharing and dispelled many preconceived ideas they had about each other. It was extremely helpful.

3. Live Out Our Lifestyle Values
   People are bonded together by their shared values. Any strong organisation, whether a business company or a local church, has core values to which its members subscribe. God has given WEC a clear set of core values which are reflected in the ethos of the mission. This book is an attempt to expound and illustrate those values. The common commitment to our organisational objectives (our commission) and to our shared convictions draw us together. But it is our lifestyle values, clearly defined since the early years of WEC, which are the key to unity. These, encapsulated in four single words, are holiness, sacrifice, faith, fellowship.

   'We need,' says Dieter Kuhl, 'to be united in our WEC ethos and core values but must give freedom in practice and patterns as far as can be biblically justified.' The outworking of those values may be different in method in various cultural contexts. For example, an Asian may only be comfortable resolving a conflict with a co-worker through using an intermediary, whereas an American would probably prefer direct confrontation. As long as fellowship is restored and maintained, the procedure is not so important provided it is done with a heart of humility and love.

4. Celebrate Our Differences
   The multi-faceted nature of the body of Christ is a cause for celebration. 'We thank the Lord that He has given us many wonderful gifts but one heart with a single purpose for God,' wrote one member of a multicultural team in Asia. An African team member admitted, 'We learned to appreciate the Dutch habit of coffee and cake after church on Sunday. We laughed about our differences.'

   Actively discovering and enjoying the differing aspects of our rich cultural diversity enriches our lives together. Some teams have used a slot at the annual conference for members to present something from their own culture. One team with seventeen different cultures did a survey among their members. They used this as a basis for understanding one another's values, attitudes and social norms. The exercise proved most enlightening and helpful.

The underlying truth

Ken Roundhill, a veteran missionary to Japan, said this at a WEC leaders' conference: 'When there is a deep work of the Cross in the hearts of both foreign missionary and national, all barriers go.'

Dr. Dieter Kuhl, in his 1996 thesis on Internationalisation, wrote: 'In our research, no evidence could be found for an increase in WEC's annual resignation rate that could possibly be due to multiculturalism. In actual fact, this rate has remained amazingly steady at below three per cent.'

Not wrong, just different

Young-Choon Lee

One time during the early years of our team, we discussed whether we should have a team celebration at Easter. Some members (Europeans) expressed quite clearly that they didn't really want to have one. For some reason I got upset and reacted rather strongly to this, and our team members were quite baffled by my reaction. Over time it had piled up; it seemed to me that all considerations began with 'I' rather than 'we', and it seemed so individualistic and selfish from my perspective.

I am an Asian and come from a society where group considerations usually take precedence over the individual's. Generally speaking, in my culture, the individual must first try to sense where the group is going and then try to accommodate to the group's decision even when he does not feel like it or it is inconvenient for him. Team spirit is maintained and built up by flowing together as one whether in ministry or relationships. As much as possible, we try to avoid referring to 'my time', 'my space' or 'my ministry'. It seemed to me that there was no true team spirit in our team when members were so vocal about personal likes, dislikes and preferences.

As I vented my frustration, team members proceeded to explain that although they had expressed their personal feelings on an issue, it didn't necessarily mean that it was a fixed conclusion – it was just the beginning of a discussion and coming to a consensus. They said that each one should be allowed to express openly what he felt so that the team could reach a decision which everyone could accept and follow. To be honest, I can't say that I was totally convinced at the time. However, with the passage of time, I have come to realise that it is a different way – not a wrong way – of approaching an issue, and that it also works!

There are strengths and weaknesses in each approach. The strength in our approach is that we automatically strive to put the interests of the team above personal preferences so that it is easier to move forward as a team. However, there is a danger that if personal feelings and frustrations are suppressed too much they may, at times, be expressed in an unhealthy way. The strength in the European (or western) approach is that it allows individuals to voice their opinions and thus bring everything out in the open for discussion. Everyone feels free to say what he thinks. The weakness of this approach is that it can sometimes hurt people in the process and that sometimes it may be very difficult to reach a decision.

Over the years, through many struggles and conflicts, our team has come to recognise our cultural differences and we have worked at relating to one another and being sensitive to our differences. This doesn't come naturally, of course, and is often a struggle. We don't want to do something that seems unnatural to us, but through this process we learn to die to ourselves. We are grateful that we have learnt to see that there are other ways (sometimes better than ours) of seeing and doing things. It enriches us and makes us that much more culturally sensitive to our national brothers and sisters.

14

Seeking and Finding

Patrick Johnstone

Core Value: *We recognise the importance of research and responding to God's direction for advance.*

Research is an integral part of our history

Research is woven into our beginnings. In every major forward move of WEC information about the need of peoples who do not have the light of the gospel has been used by the Holy Spirit to push us ever onwards to reach them. Our leaders, from C.T. Studd onwards, have either been researchers themselves or consulted researchers whom they have sought out and drawn into their intimate circle. In 1961 WEC was unique in the world of missions when it started an International Research Office in which the researcher was an integral part of the leadership team. I am convinced that our commitment since 1913 to applied research is one of the major factors that has kept us true to the first objective in our *Principles and Practice,* namely:

> To fulfil as speedily as possible the command of our Lord Jesus Christ in Matthew 28:18-20 and Acts 1:6-11, by a definite attempt to evangelise the remaining unevangelised peoples on earth before His return. *Ps&P Section Three - 1.*

It was Hudson Taylor's impassioned pleas for the need of China's unevangelised inland provinces that launched C.T. Studd and the others of the Cambridge Seven into mission in 1885. Later it was Karl Kumm's earnest challenge for a chain of mission stations across the Sahel to stop the advance of Islam southwards that led to the founding of the Sudan United Mission in 1904 and the initiation of many new advances across Africa soon after. Studd himself, though broken in health, was one of those who responded. In 1911 he was called by God into an arduous survey of South-west Sudan down to the borders of the Belgian Congo. The inland forests of the Congo were then closed to Protestants. When the opening of the Congo came in 1913, CT was off like a shot to the heart of Africa. It was there, at a place called Kilo, that WEC was founded, and it was also there that God gave the vision encapsulated in our first objective given above. In 1915, Studd wrote a booklet entitled *Christ's Etceteras* that was widely distributed. In this he laid out the fundamental principles of what would become WEC:

> Its method is to search and find out what parts of the world at present remain unevangelised, and then by faith in Christ, by prayer to God, by obedience to

the Holy Ghost, by courage, determination, and by supreme sacrifice to accomplish their evangelisation with the utmost dispatch.

Research was the means by which the various 'Heart' missions of WEC's early days were started – the Heart of Amazonia Mission (later to become the work of the Unevangelised Fields Mission), the Heart of Arabia Mission (the early workers moved out of WEC, but Arabia was picked up again forty years later) and the Heart of Asia Mission (the beginnings of our long passion for Tibetan peoples).

It is not surprising that when Norman and Priscilla Grubb returned to Britain in 1931 they should show similar vision. They, under God, became the re-founders of WEC after the upheavals of the events surrounding the death of CT. Norman was avid in his searching for news of unevangelised peoples and areas. He pounced on travellers and missionaries to prise from them what information he needed. He absorbed and applied the research of others. One of those was his brother, Sir Kenneth Grubb, once a missionary with WEC in Amazonia, and later one of the foremost missionary researchers in the years before and after World War II. He was also editor of the series of *World Christian Handbooks* published between 1947 and 1967. Grubb travelled much, visiting many WEC fields and later made this remarkable statement (my emphasis):

> My primary links with these many fields had been in first **gleaning the information of these areas that needed entry**, often through the World Dominion Surveys published by my brother Kenneth.

No wonder that despite worldwide depression and a world war the number of fields increased markedly during the years of Norman's inspired leadership. For he considered every exposure of an unevangelised area or people as a specific commission for WEC to seriously consider entry. No wonder we are running out of countries and even peoples totally untouched by mission agencies!

Norman could not do much of the actual research, so he drew to him those who could. The most significant was Leslie Brierley whose story is told below. The strategic surveys made by Leslie, in 1944-45 and 1959-61, galvanised WEC into making forward moves to many fields around the unevangelised world.

In 1977 Norman scoured WEC to find a successor to lead the International Research Office, but ultimately needed to go outside WEC and take the daring risk of inviting workers from another mission – myself and Jill, missionary evangelists with the Dorothea Mission in Southern Africa. We were also researchers, I having already written the first edition of *Operation World*. WEC leaders agreed to this proposal, and the transfer took place in 1979.

During my time as International Research Secretary I was privileged in being at the heart of two major new articulations of our first objective, in the launch of the STEP (Strategy To Every People) advance in 1984, and in 1996 the RUN (Reach the Unevangelised NOW) advance. This projected us into the biggest expansion of the work in our history as well as the biggest increase in member nationalities and a wider diversification of our spiritual ministries.

Research and its impact on WEC

Our history demonstrates that research has been challenging, invigorating and fruitful.

New vision precipitates change

Because research has been integral to the leadership of WEC, there has been that willingness to change direction, develop new ministries, take risks for God and to make necessary structural adaptations and changes to contain the new vision. As new wine has been given new wineskins, WEC has not exploded and collapsed, but grown. New visions rejuvenate. The advances of WECers into the Ouaddai in Chad or the Senegal River Valley on Mauritania's border were to some of the most inhospitable regions on the face of the earth. Wars, lack of supplies, extreme heat and dust and unresponsive peoples did not deter our workers from sticking it out, and now infant churches are coming into being. The development of our Central Asian work began seven years before the collapse of Communism in 1989-90; some mission leaders thought us mad to recruit for the Turkic peoples of that region, but when the opening came a team was already in preparation.

New vision generates new recruits

People are attracted to a new challenge – even today. Look back over our WEC history since 1945: it is interesting to see how new vision generates new recruits. This is shown dramatically in the graph below:

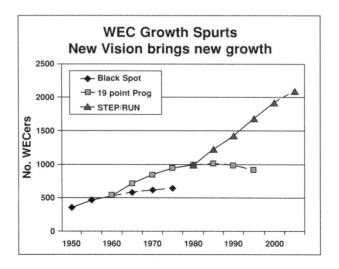

The launching of a new vision for the unevangelised gave the growth spurts which followed.

The STEP advance stimulated more creative approaches to countries and peoples not easy to reach. We developed the concept of Trans-National Fields (TNFs) for Arab, Turkic and East Asian peoples. While complicated and, at times, painful, this innovative creativity led to rapid recruitment even though we had to keep a low profile. These TNFs, in turn, are spawning a whole new generation of fields in countries which are not normally considered open for mission work. When we gathered all the statistics of WEC for the 1996 Leaders' Conference it became apparent that these new fields were our major growth area. It is not without reason we call these countries Creative Access Nations or CANs. So, comparing the number of WECers in these CANs to the FANs (Free Access Nations) we see that soon the majority of WECers will be serving in the former.

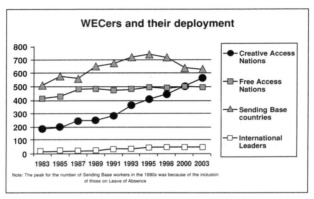

One of the spin-offs has been the remarkable increase of recruitment from newer sending countries around the world. This is a worldwide phenomenon. Asian, Latin American and African missionaries are becoming a significant component of the missionary work force. This graph shows the growth in numbers of non-western WECers since 1970:

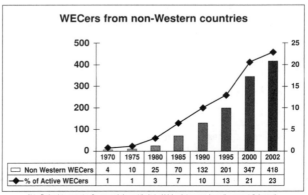

WEC research and its impact on world evangelisation

C.T. Studd bequeathed to us a generosity of spirit in helping others with a similar vision. Studd never wanted to replace the work of other churches and missions but rather to supplement them, so in 1915 he called the new mission 'Christ's Etceteras' or a 'Supplementary Worldwide Evangelisation Society'. The outworking of this giving of ourselves has been exciting. WEC's research therefore became a platform of service to the whole church.

Norman Grubb's global ministry and writings kindled vision in many directions and through his inspiration other missions such as Christian Literature Crusade and Bethany Fellowship came into being.

When I was invited to join WEC in 1978 I came with the baggage of an already published *Operation World* and the 'threat' that this would be followed by subsequent editions with all the time-consuming effort and research needed to write them. Probably over one and a half million copies of the book have been distributed in ten or so languages – remarkable for a missiological book loaded with facts for challenging Christians to intercession! This book has become a vital tool in the rapidly developing non-western missions movement, for it has provided an inexpensive source of information otherwise inaccessible in most countries. This was especially true of the Portuguese, Spanish and Korean editions.

During the 1980s I was heavily involved in the Lausanne Movement and the development of the whole concept of unreached peoples, and then in the 1990s with the AD 2000 and Beyond Movement with its goals of mobilising missions around the world to target and reach the remaining unevangelised peoples on earth. The hard work carried on in our Research Office has contributed much to the concepts, terminology and listings regarding the peoples now being reached. We therefore look to the future, encouraged and confident that the research task of finding the peoples that have never heard is virtually complete.

Into the future

And now we stand on the threshold of a new era with my stepping down as International Director for Research and the transfer of responsibility to Richard and Evelyn Hibbert who are setting up the International Department for Equipping and Advance (IDEA). Building on all that has been accomplished, IDEA is now serving as a catalyst for finding ways to finish the task more quickly and effectively. Researching and discovering Holy Spirit inspired strategies for planting and multiplying churches among the unreached peoples is the new priority. There is still much to do, and a decision was taken at our International Conference in 2002 to work towards the deployment of 150 viable church planting teams in the next six years. *Operation World* will continue under the oversight of a younger Canadian WECer, Jason Mandryk, and we believe it will continue to be a catalyst to WEC and the worldwide church.

The plodder and the prodder

Stewart Dinnen

Leslie Brierley was one man who had a profound influence on the development of WEC from the 1940s to 70s.

With a burden for the country then known as Portuguese Guinea, he tried hard to get permanent residence there but was unsuccessful. He had to remain in neighbouring Senegal but made an exploratory trip into Portuguese Guinea. While there, he became friendly with Bessie Fricker, who had obtained a residence permit. (Her story is told in *Going for God*, by Betty MacIndoe.) The Portuguese government was unhappy about Leslie's presence. It was wartime and Portugal was trying to maintain a semblance of neutrality. Leslie was given twenty-four hours to leave the country. There was a British warship in port and he was taken by it to Freetown in Sierra Leone (a British colony) where he worked in intelligence for the British government. Bessie later joined him there and they were married.

Forever a researcher and explorer, he eventually compiled a fifty-page survey on missiological matters in the colony and sent it to Norman Grubb. Norman immediately recognised his talent for research and, when Leslie was released by the British government, commissioned him to do a survey of unevangelised peoples. This he did while in London awaiting the opening of Portuguese Guinea. It was known as the Black Spot Survey and its impact was significant, with recruits coming forward for these areas.

Eventually the door opened and Leslie and Bessie worked in Portuguese Guinea for some years. They returned to the UK so that Leslie could continue his research ministry. Probably his most telling contribution was the work in preparing what became the Nineteen Point Programme which dealt with unreached areas within or near WEC fields in Africa, the Middle East and Asia. This was accepted by the leaders' conference in 1961, and its effect on recruitment was far-reaching as the challenge of these areas was presented to the churches in our sending bases.

As well as these surveys, Leslie's restless mind was forever seeking new strategies for reaching the lost and nurturing new churches. He was an inveterate plodder and prodder! One plan was for WEC to have a 'Barnabas' ministry to national churches, encouraging them to form Centres of Fellowship Worldwide. Into these information from the Research Office could be fed to help them develop their own mission strategies.

Another idea of his was Cassette Circles Worldwide – clubs for illiterates who would meet to listen to gospel and teaching cassettes prepared in their own languages.

When he handed over the reins of WEC Research to Patrick Johnstone in 1979, he turned his hand to setting up the Koinonia Information Service and produced a magazine called *Look*, then later, a slightly different broadsheet called *The Wider Look*.

WEC owes a huge debt of gratitude to Leslie, a man with a restless, inquiring, innovative mind, and a determined and indefatigable spirit.

15

Getting It All Together – Together
Philip Wood with Stewart Dinnen

Core Value: *We believe in full participation and oneness in decision-making.*

Workers in control

A basic practice in WEC is that those responsible for the implementation of a decision should participate in the decision-making process.

Norman Grubb had quite radical ideas about how a mission should be governed: he hated the thought that a board sitting in London should have any say in how the work on a field should be carried out. In actual fact, he quickly dispensed with the board and instituted the policy that 'the workers govern the work'.

The outworking of this was that each field, once established, was able to determine its own course of action. This applied to the sending bases as well. The one proviso made was that we all worked within the guidelines laid down in our *Principles and Practice*.

How does this work? Suppose an overseas field starts to be concerned for an unreached people group within its area. The leader will have some preliminary discussion with his field committee, and at conference time will raise the matter with all the workers. He will share what information he has, possibly including the result of any research that has been done, and make his proposals. After prayer, every aspect of the matter will be thoroughly discussed such as personnel needed, strategy, resources and timing. There will be another time of prayer, spreading the whole situation before the Lord and seeking to be sensitive to the leading of the Holy Spirit. After that there will be more discussion as the leader seeks to discern when a consensus seems to be coming through.

The crucial verse in scripture is 'Let the peace of God be the umpire in your hearts' (Colossians 3:15, free translation). To Norman Grubb, voting on an issue was anathema. 'Voting divides; the Spirit unites', he would say. So the key in WEC decision-making is sensitivity to the Holy Spirit.

We focus on clarity not the clock

We refuse to be governed by the clock. If an impasse is reached, a wise leader will probably say, 'Let's sleep on it.' That is code for, 'Let's take it to the Lord individually overnight.' Normally the solution comes the next day. We do have a proviso that if there is serious dissent over any issue no decision will be made without a day of prayer and fasting.

Teams, of course, need not work in isolation: regional directors are invariably present at important strategy discussions and will gladly give advice. Senior leaders in the International Office are often called upon for their views, frequently being invited to attend important consultations. While we truthfully affirm the independence of teams, there is a healthy interdependence in the workings of the mission.

Personal conviction or team guidance

Dr. Philip Wood, a WEC surgeon working in Africa, and former leader of the Canadian sending base, describes his experiences in decision-making:

I find it very comforting and reassuring that as I work within the body of Christ I don't need to make all the decisions. Each of us has been placed in a larger company, be it a church group, Bible study group, missionary team, a husband and wife couple, or just a team of two sent out to witness. No, you don't make all the decisions by yourself. You can expect that the fellowship will offer direction and if this does not correspond to what you feel then you have no mandate to press ahead.

Many situations where we need guidance are extremely complex. When I first arrived in Africa I was tempted to make all kinds of changes. There seemed to be so much paternalism, and it appeared to me that senior missionaries were not listening to the nationals. The national church wanted to get into all kinds of development projects; some looked good, others not so good. The missionaries reasoned that however good a project may appear, that if too much stress is placed on the development of better physical conditions, there could be a severe curtailment of spiritual ministry. I believe my intense sympathy with the local Africans was a form of culture shock. Only later did I appreciate the complexity of the situation and appreciate that my answers were far too simplistic. Through bitter experience the team had much to teach me and it would have been foolhardy to let one individual start a major project without its backing.

Many development projects have been very successful, but unless the whole team is involved from the start it is all too easy for distance to come between the group and the individual with the vision. A coffee project did very well for a year or so under the supervision of two enthusiastic missionaries but when they left the field no one else was prepared to take the scheme on. The team had never owned or adopted this as one of its projects. There are problems when a team is not behind the activities of its members. Nationals become wary of expatriate or expert advice if all the benefits that are suggested at the start do not materialise. Donor agencies lose confidence in a church or mission if the long-term aims of a project are not reached. For the long-term success of any project the starting point is agreement by the team on its worth.

The safeguard of team consent is crucial. If we have the mind of Christ we will be unanimous in knowing that this is the direction we should take.

When a small team of missionaries was re-establishing work in Equatorial Guinea, one member was sure she had had a prophecy that she would be protected against malaria. Consequently she went against mission policy by not taking medicines to ward off the disease. Some six months later she died of malaria and most of the Christians saw this as a definite deception of Satan to weaken the new team.

I don't mean to imply that group decisions are always right. One couple was unanimously elected to leadership in one of our sending bases but relinquished the role after one year because they were not the right people for the job. Unanimity is a way for the whole team to own a decision. This brings strength and results in commitment to agreed decisions.

The fact that guidance can come to a group is beautifully illustrated in Acts. It was while a group of leaders in Antioch was worshipping and fasting that guidance was given for Barnabas and Saul to be commissioned for their first missionary journey (Acts 13:2). Following this, we find the church deciding on questions as to how Judaic law applied to Gentiles (Acts 15:22-32). Later, all of Paul's company concluded that God had guided them through a vision given to Paul (Acts 16:10).

Choosing new leaders

Evan Davies

At the International Leaders' Conference held at Rehe, Germany, in June 2002, we were faced with the challenge of electing new International Directors. The normal procedure in WEC is to ask for nominations from all WEC leaders worldwide and then to submit the shortlist to the fields for consideration. The whole process can take up to eighteen months in an organisation which works on every continent and in some very remote places. Prior to the conference the procedure had been followed and one couple had been nominated. However, in April they felt very clearly that they had to withdraw their names. What was to happen now?

Initial enquiries were made but the picture was not at all clear. So, when the conference started, we were faced with the challenge of identifying possible candidates, listening to them, having quality time with God and reaching a unanimous conclusion.

Two possible couples were identified whose qualifications were similar. Significant times were scheduled for prayer by the conference and by WEC members and supporters around the world. The candidates gave testimony to the way God had led them and what they hoped for with regard to the future of WEC. A question and answer time was held followed by a period of prayer.

After the candidates withdrew, there was an open time of sharing among the 140 delegates. Soon it became obvious that everybody seemed to be saying the same thing. While all appreciated both couples who were standing as candidates, there were expressions from all around the conference hall that Trevor and Jenny Kallmier were to be the new leaders. When Louis Sutton, as chairman, asked if there were any who wished to speak against this, there were none. We all acknowledged that in such a hugely diverse gathering, with people from all denominational and national backgrounds, God had led us to a unanimous conclusion. This is the Lord's doing and it is marvellous in our eyes!

16

Leading Means Serving

Mike O'Donnell

Core Value: *We value servant leaders who wait on God for vision and direction.*

'I'm the plumber'

The new candidate had just arrived at Camp Hill, the venerable US WEC headquarters. As he emerged from his car he was met by a tall, thin gentleman in grease-stained overalls who gave him a friendly smile, extended his hand and introduced himself: 'Hi, I'm Elwin the plumber.'

In the commotion of multiple introductions the candidate was finding it difficult to sort everyone out. As we headed off to find his accommodation he turned to me and asked, 'And who was that fellow in the overalls?'

'Oh, that was the sending base director!' I replied.

The new arrival was in shock. Here was a company executive with 200 'employees' under his command who did not hesitate to do menial tasks. He projected an attitude not of power but of service: no pretensions, no grasping at status, simply a humble desire to do whatever was necessary for the organisation to fulfil its divinely appointed ministry.

Servant leadership is different

The concept of servant leadership is radically different from the idea of leadership commonly accepted in the world in which the leader is expected to be forceful, aggressive, and ruthless. The operative word is power. In the church, on the other hand, we talk about servanthood. Indeed, we pay much lip service to service. We call our leaders 'ministers' and refer to our meetings as 'services'. But how much do we really practise servanthood?

Aware of the disciples' intense discussion on their way to Capernaum, Jesus asks them, 'What were you arguing about on the road?' (Mark 9:33-37). His question is met with an embarrassed silence. Like children caught with their hands in the cookie jar, they wait uncomfortably for the scolding. They are too ashamed to admit that their argument had concerned the pecking order among them. Unable to comprehend Jesus' inexorable march towards the cross, their chief concern is an internal power struggle.

Jesus, well aware of the drift in their discussion, gives two illustrations concerning greatness and true leadership. He reminds them that in general society, outside the rule of God, leadership is exercised in an authoritarian and autocratic manner. 'The rulers of the Gentiles lord it over them,' He declares (Mark 10:35-45). But He goes on to say that His followers are not to operate in that way. Among those who give their allegiance to Christ, 'whoever wants to become great ... must be your servant and whoever wants to be first must be slave of all.'

In contrast to the world's measure of greatness Jesus directs His disciples to the example of a little child. The child has no pretensions, no desire to put on a façade, no reputation to defend. He is straightforward, uncomplicated and trusting. Those who aspire to Christian leadership must be willing to give themselves to the least and the lowliest. The ultimate model for God's definition of greatness is, of course, the Son of Man, who came 'to serve and to give his life as a ransom for many'.

Servanthood demonstrated

On the night before His death Jesus gave an astounding and thoroughly uncultural demonstration of servant leadership (John 13:1-17). According to the custom of those times a visitor was met at the door by a servant who would proceed to wash the dusty, dirty feet of the weary traveller. This service was never performed by the host himself, but by a slave. But here, in a deliberate and symbolic act, Jesus put Himself in the place of the slave and ministered to the basic needs of His followers by humbly washing their feet. After dealing with Peter's protests and offering some comments on His action, Jesus gave this explanation: 'I have set you an example that you should do as I have done for you ... No servant is greater than his master ... Now that you know these things, you will be blessed if you do them.'

The term 'servant leadership' is in itself a bit of a paradox. It brings together two concepts that might seem to be mutually exclusive. Some would object that the leader cannot waste time and energy doing menial tasks but must actively direct the troops, ensuring that others are taking care of practical affairs while he (or she) remains free to handle strategic matters.

It could be argued that having the sending base director working on the plumbing may not be for the overall good of the team, or the best use of the leader's resources. But we must remember that we are speaking of a fundamental issue of the heart. The leader whose attitude does not allow him to stoop to perform menial tasks, who sees himself as the supreme commander giving orders to others, misses the point of the Lord's example. The biblical picture of leadership is invariably that of servanthood under His Lordship.

Candidates from Asian countries who attend the orientation course at our British headquarters often express amazement when they find the International Director or the British Director working alongside them as members of the wash-up crew. Yes, everyone takes a share in these practical tasks.

For many years I have lived in a culture where it often seems that the primary objective of the leader is to rise to the place where he no longer has to do anything at all! The executive is the one who does nothing else but boss others around. When a major fast-food chain moved into our adopted country, a friend who was hired in this new establishment was amazed at the revolutionary concepts introduced by the company. The manager was required to do every single task that he would be asking the workers under him to do – serve meals, sweep the floors, clean the toilets, everything. Some would-be managers balked at this and thereby lost this opportunity of employment. But certainly it is a very biblical concept that the leader must not ask his followers to do anything that he himself is not willing to do.

Servant leadership requires investment of time and energy. The leader must be willing to give himself to others. It means a willingness to listen and demonstrate empathy. Patience is vital. It is very inglorious. It is not dependent on the expression of gratitude by the recipient. Those we serve will not necessarily be grateful. If we then respond with resentment, we miss the fundamental point of service. Nor is it dependent on reciprocity. As Jesus pointed out, even the world does good with the expectation of receiving in kind. The true servant heart serves regardless of whether or not the service is recognised, regardless of whether or not the response is positive.

Sometimes it is relatively easy to serve God, but much more of a challenge to serve our fellow men. Nevertheless we are called to be the servant of all, in effect to see our brothers and sisters as our 'masters'. Are we really prepared to view others in that light?

Leadership styles

Throughout the history of WEC we have had some major swings in the pendulum of leadership style and theory. In the early days leadership was directive, authoritarian and autocratic. Whatever the leader said was law. The field member had a choice between unquestioned obedience or resignation. Leaders in the early years were not up for re-election every three years as now, but rather held a permanent position. This style was perhaps relevant to a pioneer ministry. Those who launched such ministries tended to be strong individuals with the unbending conviction that they knew the mind of the Lord.

After a time, however, it became evident that such leaders could be very difficult to work with. Leadership without much servanthood resulted in a high attrition rate. Stewart Dinnen describes the process of change that followed:

> With the build-up of teams, crises of fellowship arose in many of our fields; the pioneers were not necessarily good pastoral carers. So changes had to be made. No longer was the initial pioneer the automatic leader. Elections were instituted in which the rank-and-file members chose a leader every three years. The emphasis shifted to fellowship. (*You Can Learn to Lead*, Christian Focus Publications, UK.)

This development proved to be safer but progress was slower. The leader's role tended to be reduced to that of chairing the field committee and trying to gather a consensus. Sometimes the leader seemed to be nothing more than a referee between contending parties. Servanthood without leadership resulted in fields floundering, without a clear sense of direction.

Yet, at the same time, this kind of leadership fosters loyalty and the 'ownership' of the team's united efforts. As it wrestles with future policy, even the youngest worker's opinion is important. Leaders who can bring the best out of their team find their work richly rewarded, for the forward movement of the field is in a partnership of unity and with a conviction that this way has been revealed to all by God.

In recent years the pendulum has swung back to the middle. That is why we affirm the value of 'leaders who wait on God for vision and direction'. The leaders must be allowed to lead. They have the responsibility of making sure that the team is hearing from the Lord and moving continually towards God-given objectives. They are certainly not the sole source of vision in the team. They are not infallible. They need the input and balance that a team provides. But the team must encourage the leaders to take the initiative in strategic thinking and planning, and provide the direction that is needed.

The vision of our International Directors has set patterns for development that have resulted in a framework for future advance. By thoughtful and prayerful prodding, new strategies for regional leadership, member care, regular international conferences, and initiatives for training have emerged. Leaders have been encouraged to wait on God for direction. Goals have been set, faith initiatives entered into. New fields have been opened. Unreached people groups and cities are being targeted. Partnerships with local churches and other evangelical groups is a reality.

Be shepherds of God's flock that is under your care, serving as overseers; not lording it over those entrusted to you, but being examples to the flock (1 Peter 5:2-3).

Norman Grubb

Stewart Dinnen

Norman Grubb, WEC's first International Secretary, was a great leader – a man of faith, vision, tenacity and drive – yet he had the heart of a servant.

When he travelled around Britain taking meetings, he would stay in the homes of WEC supporters. They were often amazed when, after a meeting in the lounge where a cup of tea was served, he would be found in the kitchen washing the dishes.

He served people by being intensely interested in them and by being prepared to spend precious time listening to them and giving encouragement and counsel. He maintained a voluminous correspondence with workers and leaders all over the world, advising and encouraging them to hold on and trust for great things.

When I was working alongside him in the USA headquarters, he said to me, 'Come and see me any time – the door is always open.' And when I did seek him out he would simply push away the pile of papers on his desk, turn round, and give me his complete attention.

One Canadian worker remembers a situation when a member of his family was seriously ill in a very distant part of the country. Norman, finding that this man was short of cash, quietly gave him some of his personal money so that he could go to visit him.

When, in 1985, I told him I was compiling a book of daily readings taken from his writings, he was totally astonished that I would bother to trawl through his many books with this in mind. But as always he was encouraging and, when it was completed, he wrote an appreciative foreword for it.

Under Norman's inspirational leadership WEC grew by leaps and bounds. From a small beginning with about thirty workers on one field in 1931, it grew to a total of nearly 700 workers on twenty-eight fields and nine sending bases by the time he retired from active involvement in 1965.

Ken Booth

Evan Davies

Brought up in Australia, Ken went out to India while still in his early twenties and during his first term was elected to leadership of the Himalayan field. He worked in India for fourteen years and was then invited to return to Sydney to become the Australian Sending Base Leader. Thirteen years later he returned to Asia as one of WEC's Regional Directors.

Ken was a caring and gentle leader. People loved his openness. He was friendly and interested in everybody, whether children or adults. Friendly to all, he had no aspirations to rank or privilege. When he retired from active duty with WEC, he delighted in being available to pray with and counsel needy missionaries. Every year he and Cecily would attend the annual staff conference, not to speak or be involved in the business, but to help any WECer who needed a listening ear and an understanding heart.

He was very methodical and organised in the way he conducted business. I will always remember the simple but efficient systems he used to have files and letters to hand in the right order. He went through his lists of people to see and business to be done with patient steadiness.

He was a wise man and, in any specific situation, carefully weighed up the arguments for and against before prayerfully making his decision or helping others to come to a good conclusion.

Ken wasn't a boring person but loved to have fun with anyone. His laugh and smile were infectious. He was interested in the world around and made others feel at home as they shared their interests. He wasn't afraid to join in and get his hands dirty.

I can well remember his messages full of personal illustrations and powerful principles. He shared from his heart on a level that helped people become spiritual in a practical way. His life showed it was genuine. To me he was the epitome of godly leadership; and because he served us all so well, the message he taught has had continuing relevance.

Flora Gibson

Deanne O'Donnell

We remember Flora's first arrival in Turkey and, in particular, her ready laugh and the sparkle in her eyes. She has been a blessing to us ever since.

Her example has always been one of caring servanthood. Her leadership came out of her obedience and love for the Lord. Humbly she took on those tasks that her Saviour asked of her and fulfilled them by His grace to the great encouragement and good of others.

Flora has always been stable and dependable, sensitive to others' needs, quick to come to any worker's aid. If someone needed prayer, a word of encouragement or just a listening ear, she was available whether it was convenient for her or not. Her leadership was one of good judgment, wisdom and thoughtfulness which brought people together. She is not one to enjoy giving rebukes, but where they were necessary they were prayerfully and humbly given.

Flora is a lot of fun to be with and the kids know it too. It was a treat for the children to go to her home. She would let them make trains out of the furniture, think up games to play, and there was always something special to eat. And if you wanted a race up that hill, well, Auntie Flora was right there at the starting line and the finish line too!

Flora was always welcome in the homes of the team members, and at her home one always found warm hospitality and a sense of His Presence. She keeps a quiet heart. She can be vulnerable, tired and sometimes stressed, but she knows her Rock.

We love her and we know our gracious Lord better from seeing Him in her.

17

Freedom is Strength

Ron Perschky with Stewart Dinnen

Core Value: *We promote local and innovative strategies through decentralized decision-making.*

Do we or don't we?

When the Côte d'Ivoire field became burdened for the spiritual needs of the Barala people, it was faced with a decision: 'Do we seek to reach this tribe, or do we leave it to some other group?' One thing the field did not do and that was to ask the International Director if it was okay to go ahead! No. The field had a perfect right to make its own decision, free of any external direction. Why? Because, as a mission, we believe strongly in the development of local strategies and on-the-spot decision-making.

Of course, this does not mean that the field can do something totally outlandish, such as starting a night club in Yamoussoukro, or a supermarket in Abidjan. Everyone who joins WEC signs on the dotted line giving a commitment to work within our *Principles and Practice* which sets out clear directives about our goals and general methods.

In actual fact WEC fields can only survive by recognising the high degree of interdependence that is needed. After all, new workers have to be processed through the sending bases; the bulk of money for projects comes from the home countries; and the main sources of intercessory prayer are the home prayer groups and churches.

Free but fused

Decentralized decision-making is a form of self-government that can be defined as limited autonomy – an autonomy that is exercised within the boundaries of our *Principles and Practice* and is interdependent upon other fields, home bases, ministries and offices of the fellowship. It is not total independence. In practice it allows fields and ministries to develop their work without too much interference from outside. God reveals His will to those engaged in the immediate task. Diversity with unity of purpose is part of our ethos.

Decentralized decision-making allows each team to be free of current missiological fads and to target the group to which God is leading them, or the group they feel has priority in the local situation. It may be the rural poor, urban professionals, urban poor, an unreached people group, or a geographical area, responsive or resistant.

Missions who base their target selection on the current missiological trend may neglect a people about to respond or a group that has already been reached but found in the past to be unresponsive. Convinced it was God's place for them, a WEC team kept on working throughout the years of opposition in Colombia. Then the Protestant church exploded in that land.

Yes, we acknowledge the need of countries in the 10/40 Window, but WEC continues to reach out to the Mexicans, French and Italians as well! We have developed unique ministries in Singapore, Brazil and Korea.

Contextualization is the key

WEC does not lay great emphasis on a single 'packaged' evangelistic approach such as Evangelism Explosion, the Chronological Approach or the Cell Group method. Decentralized decision-making allows teams to formulate the most appropriate strategy.

The immediate needs of the people group can be readily identified and ministered to when freedom of choice is left to the local team. Early missionaries to Ghana saw the need of leprosy sufferers and developed the Oti River leprosarium. The Betel ministry to drug addicts and HIV patients has been a revolutionary church-planting method. Bible translation was seen as an important need in Burkina Faso. Schools, hospitals and medical training were used in the Congo. A Youth Centre in The Gambia, a Bible School in Ghana, a Missionary Training College in Brazil, and the gospel broadsheets (*Bientôt*, *Booyataa*, *Cedo*, *Der Weg*, *Soon*, *Upesi*) which meet the needs of the newly literate, are but some of the innovative ministries that have developed out of on-the-spot initiatives.

Worship styles, forms of government, buildings, giving, prayer, methods of Bible study are shaped by the local team in conjunction with local believers. We are not out to impose uniformity of church life.

Political pressures inspire ingenious plans

Many of the peoples of this world have remained unreached because religious and political systems have prevented the traditional missionary approach. WEC teams are free to develop innovative means both to penetrate restricted access nations and to remain in them. This can mean taking a secular job like teaching, starting a business, enrolling in a college, medical work, researching, touring, setting up aid and relief work, representing companies, and taking degree courses one after another.

All this has only been possible because workers have the freedom to take the initiative and to step outside the traditional role. This would have been impossible had it been imposed on them by idealists living in the religious freedom of the sending base.

How decentralization works

While our *Principles and Practice* govern broad issues such as acceptance, orientation, financial policy, organisation and so on, they do not give detailed guidance on how teams should be set up locally. That is dependent, for example, on the type of services being given, the capacity and maturity of workers, and the stage of development reached by the national church. In some fields workers function in a number of small teams and in others they are widely scattered. In a number of fields the national church has a strong voice on the placement of missionaries and the nature of their ministries.

There is a strong emphasis on maintaining a close-knit fellowship in field teams. Members meet together at least once a year and possibly more than that. A representative field committee meets regularly with the leader, and the leader places a high priority on visiting and giving pastoral care to team members.

Members thus discover what leadership responsibility entails and this enhances the election process when that time comes around. WEC does not usually look outside its ranks for new leaders – they emerge from within the fellowship.

The flexibility inherent in local decision-making helps towards maintaining good relationships with national churches, and sensitivity to local issues makes it possible to give quick responses to problem situations.

Then, the best possible pattern for church-mission relationships can be developed when leaders are aware of church preferences. For instance, for many years the church in Japan wanted the mission to be fully integrated so that missionaries and national workers were interchangeable. In Thailand mission and church retain their own individual identity but work in co-operation. In Burkina Faso a close partnership arrangement exists.

There are dangers, too

Of course, there are inherent dangers in this system. Fields can become myopic and introspective, lacking in a caring attitude for other parts of the WEC body. There is also the possibility that they try to 'reinvent the wheel' when it comes to working out church-mission relationships and giving guidance about national church constitutions. It is quite possible that another field has just solved similar problems and could easily give good advice.

How can pitfalls be avoided?

Evan Davies gives us some answers:

Regional Directors serve as consultants to a group of fields and are able to pass on advice and lessons that they personally have learned, or that other fields in the region have discovered. The International Department for Equipping and Advance keeps the global perspective before us, and the International Training Director provides advice and training seminars for leaders and potential leaders. The International Office keeps the WEC 'body' together, relating to all fields, sending bases, Co-ordinating Council and Leaders' Council.

A massive interactive process takes place every six years when all leaders meet to discuss strategy, policy, problems and world trends. Regional conferences are also held under the leadership of Regional Directors. But in all of this, the self-governing status of fields is upheld and policy decisions affecting the fields are left to the team members.

Of course all this is based on trust in the Holy Spirit; and we trust the Spirit in each member to guide us personally and corporately.

A field initiative that paid off

Stewart Dinnen

Our original thrust in Brazil was evangelistic work and subsequent church nurture in the province of Minas Gerais. The workers were keen to learn from the success of other churches in their area, so when they saw tremendous growth in a church in the town of Belo Horizonte, they decided to commit a couple to working with it in order to learn and replicate its methods. The church had been started by a pastor who advertised in the local newspaper, offering a free Christian counselling service based on biblical truth. The response was overwhelming. He would give immediate advice over the phone and then invite his contacts to attend his church in downtown Belo.

The field decided to try out this strategy in Montes Claros, 500 km to the north. The couple who had learned the technique in Belo pioneered it there.

Again, the response was immediate and soon many were being counselled but, realising there were several evangelical churches in the town, the couple wisely decided to funnel contacts into them. Soon the pastors were overwhelmed with the need to disciple these new converts, and eventually asked WEC to start an evening Bible school to help them. This functioned successfully for several years until its growth reached the stage when the logical step was a full-time Bible school with a missionary emphasis. Today, numbers of Brazilians who have been trained in this facility are serving with WEC and other Christian ministries.

The field has also become a sending base, and has been greatly used in inspiring missionary vision in churches and in stimulating the start of indigenous Brazilian missions.

18

We Go On!

Evan Davies

The job isn't finished yet!

A great company of Christians from many countries round the world are reaching out, showing the love of Jesus, preaching the Good News of the Kingdom, discipling new believers, planting new churches and recruiting others to finish the task. WEC is a small part of that company committed to obeying Christ's command to make Jesus known in every place and among people who have no idea of this liberating power, a power that can give them a life beyond their dreams.

Have we changed?

Of course we have. We keep reviewing our principles and methods and listening to God for any new directives He has for today and tomorrow. Our guidelines are not meant to be tramlines to restrict us from moving along divine tangents. We have introduced new structures that have blessed us, given better member care and shared the load of leadership more evenly. We are now increasingly multicultural and are trying to learn the lessons of being truly international. We keep our goals clear so that the evangelism of the remaining unevangelised is our over-arching objective. But in it all, as C.T. Studd said, 'We seek to keep our administrative structures simple. We see the danger of binding the Spirit in red tape so that we virtually ask Him to sit in a corner while we get on with the work.'

What has been accomplished?

Many thousands have come to faith in Christ, whole societies have been impacted with loving care in Jesus' name, churches have been planted and hundreds recruited to pray, give and go. It will only be around the throne, as we read in Revelation 5 and 7, that we will see the real picture: the Congolese who believed (and oh, how they suffered), the Burkinabes who stood against the power of the fetish, the tens of thousands who prayed and gave, the Brazilians who will joyfully shout their praises, the Middle Eastern Christians who have come out of great trial and danger, the children who were loved into the Kingdom, the millions who heard of Jesus through the broadsheet ministries, those who came to know Jesus over the Internet, the Fijians, Indonesians and

Japanese who came to faith, and the hundreds of converted drug addicts made clean by the blood of the Lamb. Was it worth it? A thousand times yes!

Dieter Kuhl has said, 'To go forward we must go deeper.' Ron Perschky has warned, 'It's great to accept a vision but there is a cost to pay, for our vision will thrust us into zones that are uncomfortable and we will go into a period of unprecedented hostility for we are treading into areas that Satan has controlled.'

We cannot draw back. Refine our methods and review our strategies, certainly, but to retreat – never! Jesus has given His marching orders and has not rescinded them. He is determined to build His church and has promised to be with us to the end of the age.

The words of William Booth, founder of the Salvation Army, continue to inspire us:

While women weep, I'll fight; while little children go hungry as they do now, I'll fight; while men go to prison, in and out, in and out, I'll fight; while there yet remains one dark soul without the light of God, I'll fight – I'll fight to the very end!

So, too, do the words of C.T.Studd, our founder:

If Jesus Christ be God and died for me then no sacrifice can be too great for me to make for Him!

Contributing Writers

John Bardsley A school teacher from Queensland, Australia, John joined WEC in 1972. He served first on the staff of WEC's Missionary Training College (MTC) in Tasmania, then in various states in Australia until he joined the International Research Office in the UK. He is now International Director for Prayer.

Graham Chalker Graham is from Australia and in 1984 went to Côte d'Ivoire with his wife. They were involved in an evangelism and discipling ministry until Graham contracted motor neurone disease. They now serve on the staff of WEC's Sydney base.

Jonathan & Linda Chamberlain The Chamberlains are from the UK and went to Indonesia in 1975. From 1989 they led WEC's developing Singapore base until they moved to the International Office as Deputy International Directors in 1999.

Jeanette Cooke Converted in Tasmania through the ministry of students at WEC's MTC, Jeanette eventually joined the staff there in 1975. In 1986 she and her husband transferred to the Netherlands to assist in the commencement of the European MTC.

Tineke Davelaar Tineke came from the Netherlands and in 1972 went to Iran. When Christian workers were expelled from that country, she returned to the Netherlands and developed the WEC small group Bible study ministry (Geared for Growth) there. Later, she worked in Pakistan and Central Asia. She was appointed to work as joint Candidate Director with Janny Riemersma in the Dutch sending base, but died in November 2003 after a short illness.

Evan & Jenny Davies Evan, whose parents were WEC missionaries, comes from the UK, and Jenny is from Australia. In 1964 God called them to the staff of WEC's MTC in Tasmania where they served for twenty-seven years. In 1991 they transferred to the International Office, first as Deputy International Directors and then as International Directors.

Stewart Dinnen   Stewart and his wife are from Scotland and felt God's call to join the staff of WEC's MTC in Glasgow (now closed) in 1949. In 1960, after a period on the staff at WEC's sending base in the USA, they became Principals of the MTC in Tasmania. After eighteen years in leadership, they were appointed as International Directors for Training and eventually International Directors. Stewart died in 2003.

Rollie Grenier   Rollie and his wife come from Canada and Colombia. They went to Spain in 1992 and eventually transferred to Equatorial Guinea where they are involved in leadership and a Bible training ministry.

Patrick Johnstone   Patrick is from the UK. After working in Southern Africa with the Dorothea Mission, he was invited to become WEC's International Director for Research in 1979. Well known as the author of *Operation World*, he has an international ministry.

Phyllis Kilbourn   Phyllis left the USA in 1967 to serve in Liberia. Her interest in children's education took her to Kenya. Her concern for the children traumatised by war in Liberia and elsewhere led to the start of Rainbows of Hope – a WEC ministry to children in need.

Young-Choon Lee   Young-Choon Lee is from Korea. He and his wife went to Mongolia in 1993 where they are now the field leaders. Young-Choon has also been Principal of the Mongolian Bible College.

Dave Macmillan   Dave and his wife, who come from South Africa, went to Thailand in 1980. They became field leaders but now exercise an international speaking role from their home in Chiangmai.

Patrick McElligott Patrick grew up in London, UK, and went to Japan with his wife in 1972. He now is a university chaplain and itinerant speaker in the UK.

Mike O'Donnell   Mike comes from the USA and went to the Near East in 1971. With his wife, he was involved in evangelism, Bible translation and in the development of a large field. He is now Regional Director for Central Asia.

Ron Perschky

Ron is from the UK and in 1972 went to Thailand in response to God's call. Eventually he and his wife, Margery, served as WEC's Regional Directors in South Asia. Since 1999 they have been Principals at the MTC in Tasmania.

Jim & Judy Raymo

The Raymos come from the USA. They served on staff at the MTC in Tasmania during 1987 and then became Candidate Directors in the USA. Since 1998 they have been US Sending Base Leaders.

Janny Riemersma

Janny is from the Netherlands and joined WEC in 1974. She has served in Kalimantan, Indonesia and then in Central Asia. In 2002 she was appointed as joint Candidate Director (with Tineke Davelaar) in the Netherlands.

Helen Roseveare

Helen, a medical doctor, is well known through her many books and speaking tours. From the UK, she went to Congo in 1951. She experienced the trauma of the Civil War but later returned to the Congo to help develop a medical training centre.

Neil Rowe

Neil has handled a variety of roles in WEC. In 1955 he joined the staff of the MTC in Glasgow and then, in turn, became the Director of WEC Press UK, Manager of Bulstrode (the UK sending base property), UK Director, Regional Director for Africa and then the Middle East. He and his wife now have an itinerant ministry.

Dore Schupak

Dore is from the USA and joined WEC in 1986. He served first in the Indian sub-continent and then moved to Central Asia where he and his wife have been leaders of a fast developing network of fields.

Louis & Susan Sutton

The Suttons come from the USA and have served in Chad since 1987. They have been involved in a medical ministry and as field leaders.

Mady Vaillant

Mady is from France and joined WEC in 1960 to work in Burkina Faso. Following a period in leadership there, she became part of the Regional Director team in the African Regional Office.

Philip Wood   In 1973 Philip and Nancy Wood left the UK and Canada to be involved in a medical ministry in Congo. Later they worked with ELWA Hospital in Liberia. They were Canadian Sending Base Leaders for several years and have recently returned to a medical ministry in Congo.

Brian Woodford   Brian is from the UK and went to Burkina Faso in 1958. He was involved in pioneer church planting and Bible translation. Over the years he has worked in New Zealand and Ghana in Bible teaching and for several years was International Director for Training. He now teaches at the MTC in New Zealand.

Selected Bibliography

Please note: a number of these titles are out of print.

AUTHOR	TITLE	PUBLISHER	DATE
Bannister E.	*Access Without Visa*	WEC, Gerrards Cross, UK	1995
Davidson A.	*High Adventure With God*	CLC, Manila	1974
Dinnen S.	*All for the Best*	WEC, Gerrards Cross, UK	1988
	Faith on Fire	CFP, Fearn, UK	1997
	Here We Stand	WEC, Gerrards Cross, UK	1983
	Learning About Union With Christ	CFP, Fearn, UK	2000
	Real Guidance	CFP, Fearn, UK	2003
	Rescue Shop Within a Yard of Hell	CFP, Fearn, UK	1995
	Sacking the Frontiers of Hell	CFP, Fearn, UK	2000
	When I Say Move	CLC, Alresford, UK	1972
Easton W.	*Colombian Conflict*	CLC, UK	1954
Eley J.	*God's Brumby*	WEC, Australia	1982
Grubb N.P.	*After C.T. Studd*	Lutterworth, London	1939
	Christ in Congo Forests	Lutterworth, London	1945
	Continuous Revival	CLC London	1952
	C.T. Studd, Cricketer & Pioneer	Lutterworth London/CLC USA	1933
	First the Blade	WEC, London	1963
	Once Caught, No Escape	Lutterworth, London	1969
	Successor to C.T. Studd	Lutterworth, London	1949
	The Four Pillars of WEC	WEC London	1963
	The Growth of WEC	WEC, London	1963
	The Spirit of Revival	CFP, Fearn, UK	2000
	Touching the Invisible	Lutterworth, London	1960
Harverson S.	*Doctor in Vietnam*	Lutterworth, London	1968
Jewell M.V.	*Welthy's Wonderful World*	Margaret's Book Shelf, Westport, IN, USA	1984
Kullesky H.	*Travail, Triumph, Jubilee*	WEC, Fort Washington, USA	1989
Mackey R.	*God Steps In Again*	CLC, London	1973
McDermid M.	*The Adventure of Working With God*	WEC, Fort Washington, USA	2000
McElligott P.	*On Giants' Shoulders*	WEC, Gerrards Cross, UK	1991
Moules L.	*Ascent of the Inner Everest*	CLC, London	1971
	Some Want It Tough	CLC, London	1961
	Then God Stepped In	CLC, London	1963
	This Is No Accident	WEC, London	1965
Myers G.	*Learning to Forgive*	CFP, Fearn, UK	1997

AUTHOR	TITLE	PUBLISHER	DATE
Raymo J.	*Meeting Jesus in Australia*	WEC, Fort Washington	1990
	Marching to a Different Drummer	CLC, Fort Washington, USA	1996
Roseveare H.	*Give Me This Mountain*	IVP, Leicester/WEC USA	1966
	He Gave Us A Valley	IVP, Leicester/WEC USA	1976
	Living Faith	H & S, London	1980
	Living Fellowship	H & S, London	1984
	Living Holiness	H & S, London	1986
	Living Sacrifice	H & S, London	1979
	Living Stones	H & S, London	1988
Rowbotham E.	*Would You Believe It!*	WEC, Glasgow, UK	1963
Ruscoe A.	*The Lame Take The Prey*	Bethany Publishers, Minneapolis, USA	1968
Scheunemann D.	*The Holy Spirit and World Evangelisation*	Indonesian Missionary Fellowship, Malang, Indonesia	1984
Scotland T. & L.	*Voice From the Stars*	T & L Scotland, Perth, Aus.	1990
	After Voice From the Stars	T & L Scotland, Perth, Aus.	1993
Searle L.	*Going Through With God*	WEC, Fort Washington, USA	1965
Studd C.T.	*Chocolate Soldier*	WEC, UK	(1989)
	Christ's Etceteras	WEC, UK	(1988)
	Laugh of Faith	WEC, UK	Undated
	Reminiscences of Mrs C.T. Studd	WEC, UK	1930
Tait V.G.	*Attitude of Gratitude*	WEC, Fort Washington, USA	1992
Vincent E.	*No Sacrifice Too Great/ C.T. Studd and Priscilla*	STL/WEC/Kingsway, Eastbourne, UK	1988
Walker J.	*Fool and Fanatic?*	WEC, UK	Undated
Wraight P.	*On To The Summit: The Len Moules Story*	Kingsway, Eastbourne & CLC, Alresford, UK	1981

Publishers' Abbreviations

CFP	Christian Focus Publications
CLC	Christian Literature Crusade
H & S	Hodder & Stoughton
IVP	Inter-Varsity Press, UK
STL	Send The Light Publishers (Operation Mobilisation)
WEC	WEC International

WEC International has around 1800 workers drawn from over 40 countries in over 70 countries of the world. From its beginnings in the Congo in 1913 it has grown to work in many parts of the world. Evangelical and inter-denominational in outlook, WEC's ethos is based on Four Pillars of Faith, Sacrifice, Holiness, and Fellowship. WEC's commission is to bring the gospel of our Lord Jesus Christ to the remaining unevangelised peoples of the world with utmost urgency, to demonstrate the compassion of Christ to a needy world, to plant churches and lead them to spiritual maturity, and to inspire, mobilise and train for cross-cultural mission.

To help us achieve that, we have 16 Sending Bases scattered throughout the world which recruit, screen, send and help support workers. We also train missionary workers at six training institutes around the world.

WEC workers are involved in almost every type of direct outreach and support ministry related to the fulfilment of these aims. WEC's ministries range from the International Research Office that produces the prayer handbook *Operation World*, through the planting and establishment of churches, to the enabling of national missionary sending agencies in mature WEC fields.

Our Lifestyle

We fervently desire to see Christ formed in us so that we live holy lives.

In dependence on the Holy Spirit we determine to obey our Lord whatever the cost.

We trust God completely to meet every need and challenge we face in His service.

We are committed to oneness, fellowship and the care of our whole missionary family.

Our Convictions:

- We are convinced that prayer is a priority.
- We uphold biblical truth and standards.
- We affirm our love for Christ's Church, and endeavour to work in fellowship with local and national churches, and with other Christian agencies.
- We accept each other irrespective of gender, ethnic background or church affiliation.
- We desire to work in multi-national teams and are committed to effective international cooperation.
- We recognise the importance of research and responding to God's directions for advance.
- We believe in full participation and oneness in decision making.

- We value servant leaders who wait on God for vision and direction.
- We promote local and innovative strategies through decentralised decision making.
- We make no appeals for funds.

"If Jesus Christ be God and died for me, no sacrifice can be too great for me to make for Him."

C T Studd

www.wec-int.org